ARCHAEOLOGY
and Our
Old Testament
Contemporaries

THE GREAT SEA

HAZOR

SEA OF
GALILEE

GATH-HEPHER

MEGIDDO

BETH-SHEAN

DOTHAN

SAMARIA

SHECHEM

BETHEL

JAFFA

GIBEAH

JERICHO

GIBEON

JERUSALEM   QUMRAN

BETHLEHEM

TEKOA

LACHISH

KIRIATH-SEPHER   HEBRON

DEAD SEA

GERAR

SODOM

BEERSHEBA

Old
Testamen
Site

ARCHAEOLOGY
and Our
Old Testament
Contemporaries

JAMES L. KELSO
Foreword by W. F. Albright

ZONDERVAN PUBLISHING HOUSE
Grand Rapids   **Michigan**

ARCHAEOLOGY AND OUR OLD TESTAMENT CONTEMPORARIES
Copyright © 1966 by
Zondervan Publishing House
Grand Rapids, Michigan

Library of Congress Catalog Card Number 66-13691

First printing 1965
Second printing . . . . . March, 1966
Third printing . . . November, 1966

Printed in the United States of America

DEDICATION

*"To my wife,
an archaeologist
in her own right"*

FOREWORD

This book is an unusual and much needed contribution to modern Christian understanding of our Hebrew past. It is neither "fundamentalist" nor "liberal," but is written from a staunch theologically conservative point of view. No popular book of this type has ever been so well grounded in natural science and the history of technology. With a long record of excavation in Palestine behind him, the author is a reliable guide on archaeological matters.

Having been intimately associated with the author since 1926, I have learned to appreciate his outstanding qualities as a man and as an archaeologist. Like James Henry Breasted, who attributed part of his success in interpreting Egyptian medical texts to his early training as a pharmacist, so James L. Kelso has utilized his early preparation in the same field for the elucidation of technical problems in ancient ceramics and metallurgy.

Two strong currents run through this volume: a sustained atmosphere of reverence and a common-sense approach to human affairs, seasoned by flashes of wit. Personally, I find the book particularly instructive for its unexpected parallels between the Biblical and modern worlds. Humanity has indeed remained the same, and human culture has changed far less than commonly supposed.

WILLIAM F. ALBRIGHT
Professor of Near Eastern Studies
The Johns Hopkins University
Baltimore, Maryland

CONTENTS

Foreword

Fragments of the Dead Sea Scrolls under glass plates. *Photo courtesy Palestine Archaeological Museum*

Abraham, International Business Genius
and Christian Saint

Chapter I

Abraham, International Business Genius and Christian Saint

Juglets for holding olive oil (left) and perfume (right).

There are two common major mistakes in Old Testament interpretation today. One is to underestimate the God of the Old Testament and the second is to underestimate its finest people. Let us begin with the second theme. The average modern man assumes that the ancients must have been of lesser intellect than we are, since they lived so long ago. We forget that we are the heirs of the intellectuals of all the ages; and most of civilization has been simply a slow improvement in technology. Only in science can our generation be said to be intellectual beyond the normal growth pattern.

The greatest invention in all of human history was writing and the Sumerians invented that before 3000 B.C., more than a millennium before Abraham. The golden age of Greece saw more intellectuals in the one city of Athens than in any single city since that time. We pride ourselves on our mass production industry and assembly line techniques, but ancient Israel of the days of Isaiah and Jeremiah was already practicing such methodology. The writings of the prophets show the farmer abandoning his ancestral land, coming into the city and being swallowed up in the new industrial revolution. But we ourselves have failed to solve this same economic problem, although we benefit by 2500 years of experience. In ceramic techniques J. Palin Thorley, one of America's best experts in that field, said he could have lived back with those old potters and been perfectly happy for they knew all the techniques of the trade. By Joseph's time ceramics and metallurgy were at an industrial and artistic peak in Palestine not again to be matched even in Hellenistic and Roman times. Like ourselves the ancients were quick to develop their new inventions and discoveries and to master many of their facets. The Palestinians did this with ceramics, the Sumerians with copper alloys and the Romans with cement. The world's first fortified city was Jericho of 7500 B.C. and its stones were cut to shape several thousand years before metals were known.

This is no attempt to exaggerate the work of the ancients, for like ourselves they could be 5000 years ahead in one field of science and at the same time miss other factors in that field that seem to us to be more simple of solution. They missed the real significance of electricity although they mastered far more difficult scientific problems. The history of civilization has always had and still has both a credit and a debit page. One lists success in spite of overwhelming odds; the other notes failure in spite of an abundance of easy clues and apparent demonstrations. One of the major contributions of archaeology is its demonstration that *human nature is the same in all generations.* This is what makes history intelligible, if not always sane.

The ancients had their failures too. The Greeks were geniuses in many fields, but were a total failure in religion and the ability to live with one another. This greatest civilization of antiquity died a suicide's death because, like present day culture, it omitted God. Their theme song was our modern one, "Money, money makes the man." No people in history, however, has ever been able to serve both God and mammon. The greatest tragedy of all history was Israel, which was given God's saving revelation to pass on to all mankind; and yet Israel rejected this God and crucified her Messiah.

The ancients like the moderns were all kinds of peoples: sinners and saints, geniuses and ignoramuses, mediocre and mine-run. But in all history, it is normally the best and the worst that attract attention — most of the others simply fade out of the picture.

The Old Testament was Christ's Bible and that fact makes this book unique for any sincere intellectual of today! Every thoughtful Christian sees that modern sinners are simply duplicates of Old Testament sinners. Modern man has invented no new sins, nor has he found any remedy for sin save Jesus, the Christ — the same yesterday (Old Testament times), today (modern civilization), and tomorrow (heaven). The crucial question for each of us to ask today is this. Is my own Christian life as good as those of the best Old Testament saints? To that end let us restudy the Old Testament through the eyes of Christ.

The book of Genesis consists of two themes. The first eleven chapters are theological essays; the remainder of the book is theological biographies. The theological essays belong in a special technical field of literature which demands a broad knowledge of Semitic thought patterns, customs and manners; but the theological biographies come over rather well into an English translation. (The layman, however, must always realize that a translation is comparable to a photograph in black and white; it is only in the original text that you get a true color photograph.)

The Bible biography is an ideal pattern for the portrayal of theology as it breathes the dialogue between God and man. It denies theology the use of theory, and hammers out its doctrine on facts alone. Biblical biography is always aware of the unique grace of its God on the one hand and the earthiness and sin of man on the other hand. Yet it always insists that man is made in God's image and is redeemable. John 3:16 is the text upon which all the Old Testament as well as the New Testament is penned.

Now let us turn to the study of Abraham, the father of the faithful, who is so important to New Testament thought that he is mentioned over seventy times there, and almost half of these references are in the gospels. The archaeologist who has specialized in Abraham knows that he was an *international businessman* who lived somewhere around 1900 B.C. His sales territory reached from

Approaching Beer-sheba from the northeast. © *Matson Photo Service*

Haran near the Taurus mountains of Turkey down into Egypt; his nephew Lot also served as his agent for Arabia. Such big business demanded loans and Eliezer of Damascus was Abraham's banker; and as security for these loans Abraham adopted Eliezer and thus that lender became the legal heir. Nuzi laws of a later date show this adoptive technique still in use. In those days of international unrest such a large business enterprise as Abraham's needed its own small but efficient army; and in Genesis 14 Abraham used such commando units in Trans-Jordan for the rescue of Lot and his property. Note also that in Genesis 21:22-33 Abimelech's army had to return Beer-sheba to Abraham.

This Genesis 14 story is as modern as today. Early exegetes could never understand that military campaign since it ended in the dead-end streets of Edom and Sinai.

Today, however, we know that these two countries were major copper areas sufficiently rich for nations to fight over. It was later at Edom's Ezion-geber that Solomon built a fleet to sell copper from the same mines to the coastal cities of Arabia. Solomon, like Abraham, was a good businessman. In his day iron was replacing copper in the Mediterranean basin and Solomon, just like any modern businessman, sold his outdated product to the backward nations, i.e. down the Red Sea. In exchange he received good Arabian gold; and it is hard for a modern businessman to make a better economic exchange than did Solomon.

Abraham was a "merchant prince" whose sales territory reached from Haran to Egypt, but he concentrated especially on three areas: Palestine south of Shechem, Egypt and Arabia. We have no specific mention of the items sold by Abraham, but they were doubtless the ordinary luxury goods which were exchanged between the rich of all countries. Gold and silver jewelry, with or without precious stones as settings, was common. Precious stones themselves often served as coinage, for the rarest of them were far more valuable than gold or silver. Richly embroidered garments were sales items just as they are today between various nationalities. Clothing was so expensive in Old Testament times that it is even mentioned as booty in war. Bronze items of all kinds were luxury goods. These items would be especially profitable for Abraham as he could buy copper cheap at the mines in Edom or Sinai and transport it to Phoenicia and Syria which were then the major manufacturing centers. From there he could sell these products anywhere from Anatolia to Egypt and Arabia.

Haran was Abraham's original business capital. It

was located about halfway between the Mediterranean
coast and Nineveh. It was a miniature Chicago with trade
routes radiating in all directions. This city was a blend
of two distinct cultures, Semitic and Hurrian, and both
of these are reflected in the Genesis narrative. His father,
Terah, had worked the Ur-Haran sales territory at the time
when Ur was the most influential commercial city in the
world. The family must have been highly influential as
at least three of Abraham's ancestors (Serug, Nahor and
Terah) had cities named in their honor. Sarah was also
wealthy in her own right, for she is spoken of as a "wife-

The living room of a wealthy home in Abraham's time. *Kelso*

sister." This was a Hurrian legal term used in Haran. It identified Sarah as a member of the aristocracy of Haran.

Later Abraham concentrated on the Palestine-Egypt trade. Gerar, the commercial heart of the Palestine Negeb, became Abraham's adopted city. Such an action was necessary to give him a legal base of supplies for his Egyptian trade. Later Hebron and Beer-sheba overshadowed Gerar. Hebron became Abraham's summer capital and Beer-sheba his winter one. Hebron dominated southern Judah as is shown by David's use of it for his first capital. Beer-sheba was the key city of the eastern Negeb.

Abraham's wealth is well-demonstrated by the exorbitant price he paid for a new family cemetery in Hebron. It cost him 400 silver shekels, but for similar Palestinian real estate Jeremiah paid only seventeen silver shekels. Abraham was forced to pay this high price to the natives since he was compelled to have a cemetery at the center of the new homeland which he was founding at God's command. Note that the sale price in silver is quoted at "the current market rate," just as in international business today.

The first stop that Abraham made in Palestine was at Shechem which was a Hurrian business center related to Haran. The city was located in central Palestine with good trade routes in all directions. In both Haran and Shechem the *ass* was the sacrificial animal, not the sheep. Abraham now took over grazing rights in the virgin territory on the mountain ridge between Shechem and Hebron. (Later Jacob extended this range north to Dothan.) Only a merchant prince could control such an extended pasturage. Genesis 13:2 mentions cattle along with Abraham's capital funds in silver and gold. Like a good businessman his money was distributed in various enterprises.

His caravans always needed food and fodder and Abraham supplied both of these from his own agricultural projects.

The most unique section of his trade route was between Kadesh and Shur, i.e. through the Sinai desert. This desert road could only be used for luxury goods of light weight. Droves of sheep and cattle could not take this route for water was too scarce. This was strictly donkey terrain. The ordinary historic trade route from Palestine to Egypt followed the coast but for a brief period this secondary inland route was also used. It was abandoned shortly after Abraham's day and was not re-used until Solomon's time. This Kadesh-Shur route through the desert fits in perfectly with the fact that Abraham is called a Hebrew. In his day this word meant a *caravaneer*. These men worked the donkey pack trains that carried most of the world's commerce of that age. The largest of these donkey trains ran from 1,000 to 3,000 animals. The camel did not become cheap enough to replace the donkey until after the days of the Judges. Wagons were rare as most roads were dirt tracks. In the mountains only donkeys could be used. In the early west of America its mountain sections likewise depended on the pack train.

Sodom in Trans-Jordan was Abraham's outlet to the Arabian trade lanes. He put his nephew, Lot, in charge of this commerce. At that time the Dead Sea did not extend as far south as it does today and a direct trade route then ran between Abraham's headquarters at Hebron and Lot's branch office at Sodom. Abraham's marriage to Keturah with the consequent wide distribution of the Arabian descendants of that union demonstrates the wide expansion of Abraham's Arabian business empire (Genesis 25:1-4). See also Abraham's descendants through Ishmael (Genesis 25:12-16).

So much for Abraham, the big businessman; now to Abraham the Christian saint. The adjective "Christian" may seem confusing at first sight, but recall John 8:56, "Abraham rejoiced to see my day; and he saw it, and was glad." Although Abraham was known as the friend of God (Isaiah 41:8), the disciples of Jesus did not receive such a similar designation until passion week! Christ's definition of "friend" applies alike to Abraham, Christ's disciples and modern Christians. "Ye are my friends, if ye do the things which I command you." Also restudy Galatians 3:8, "And the scripture, foreseeing that God would justify the Gentiles by faith, preached the gospel beforehand unto Abraham, saying, In thee shall all the nations be blessed."

The greatest of all God's commandments is that we believe Him. Of Abraham we read, "He believed in God; and he reckoned it to him for righteousness" (Genesis 15:6). Here is the first basic statement of all Scripture for the doctrine of Justification by Faith, a maxim never to be improved on in the Bible, although vastly expanded and explained in the New Testament. Romans, Galatians and James all quote this Genesis 15:6.

This doctrine is seen at its best in Abraham's leaving his ancestral home at God's command and in his offering up of Isaac. In the former God asked him to violate every cherished Mesopotamian concept of what a home was; and even at death, Abraham was still without a home! "By faith he became a sojourner in the land of promise, as in a land not his own, dwelling in tents, with Isaac and Jacob, the heirs with him of the same promise; for he looked for the city which hath the foundations, whose builder and maker is God" (Hebrews 11:9-10). In antiquity the living and the dead were a common family.

Abraham's Oak near Hebron. © *Matson Photo Service*

Indeed, in the earliest times the dead were buried under the floor of the house they had lived in. This was practiced even in Ur of the Chaldees. Now God asks Abraham to separate himself from all his kin both living and dead and to initiate a new family in a new land. Ordinarily only an *outcast criminal* was treated in this manner. This is the test that God placed on Abraham at his initial call.

The Isaac episode, however, is the crux of Abraham's faith. Scholars often sneer at this story and count Abraham but another Canaanite and this but another pagan child sacrifice. But study the story carefully. Abraham has already done the impossible for a good man of his day and abandoned his old homeland only to find himself without a son by whom to establish a new homeland. Weak in faith at this point, he tried to improve on providence and begat Ishmael through Hagar, Sarah's handmaid. But God's grace could not be thwarted and in due time the promised Isaac was given. But Isaac was given only to be taken away in the tragic command, "Take now thy son, thine only son, whom thou lovest, even Isaac, and get thee into the land of Moriah; and offer him there for a burnt offering."

When Abraham's faith is equal to God's command his sacrificial knife is stayed — for God wants Abraham, not Isaac. The son is spared and God makes a startling, unique vow that "In thy seed shall all the nations of the earth be blessed; because thou hast obeyed my voice." Here is an epitome of all genuine faith; it must ultimately benefit *all* mankind. It is not simply a problem for Abraham and Isaac; its correct solution must be a blessing for *all* mankind. To accomplish this promised blessing, however, this same Mt. Moriah (Jerusalem) must ultimately see sacrifice done here! But this time it is God's Son and not the son of Abraham!

The Tomb of Abraham in the Mosque of Machpelah in Hebron.
© *Matson Photo Service*

In a certain sense Genesis anticipates the New Testament dispensation for it has no Mosaic law. God deals face to face with the patriarchs as Jesus does with His disciples. "Know therefore that they that are of faith, the same are sons of Abraham. And the scripture, foreseeing that God would justify the Gentiles by faith, preached the gospel beforehand unto Abraham, saying, In thee shall all the nations be blessed" (Galatians 3: 7-8). Like the disciples of Christ, Abraham's daily life was by no means above reproach; but Christ's grace was sufficient in both the Old Testament and the New Testament dispensation, and it is equally efficient today.

Abraham, the international business genius and Christian saint, is not only as modern as today, but in Luke 16:22 Christ even takes him over into the future

The Mosque at Hebron. *Kelso*

life. "And it came to pass, that the beggar died, and that he was carried away by the angels into *Abraham's bosom;* and the rich man also died and was buried."

* * * *

For detailed archaeological data on Abraham see W. F. Albright, *Bulletin of the American Schools of Oriental Research,* No. 163, pp. 36-54.

For more detailed theological data on all portions of the Old Testament see the author's companion volume to this book on *The Christian God of the Old Testament.* For an excellent detailed history of all the Old Testament see John Bright, *A History of Israel.* For the best geographic study of the Bible see *The Geography of the Bible* by Denis Baly. For a resume of the archaeology of Palestine see W. F. Albright, *The Archaeology of Palestine.*

Moses, History's Most
Unique Statesman

Chapter II

Moses, History's Most Unique Statesman

Examples of pottery from Joseph's time.

Abraham was a big businessman concentrating on the Palestine-Egyptian luxury trade, but his great grandson Joseph was elevated to the position of prime minister of Egypt itself. This was indeed a talented family by either ancient or modern standards. Although Joseph devoted his life to both his Israelite brothers and his adopted

Egypt, he never forgot Abraham's title deed to the promised land. "And Joseph said unto his brethren, I die; but God will surely visit you, and bring you up out of this land unto the land which he sware to Abraham, to Isaac, and to Jacob. And Joseph took an oath of the children of Israel, saying, God will surely visit you, and ye shall carry up my bones from hence" (Genesis 50:24-25). The strangest baggage Israel carried on all its forty year trek through the Sinai desert was this mummy of the prophetic Joseph.

Between the time when we close our book of Genesis and open the book of Exodus something like 400 years has elapsed. (For comparative purposes note that it is less than five centuries since Columbus discovered America.) The Israelites whom we last saw under Joseph in Genesis were special favorites of the Egyptian court. In Exodus they are now serfs of a new Egyptian dynasty, busily employed as members of the corvée building Pithom and Raamses. The first was a military depot on the Sinai frontier. It has been excavated and found to contain underground silos for the storage of grain for the army. The bricks found in some of these pits fit exactly the Biblical description — some made with straw, some with stubble and some without any vegetable matter (Exodus 1:14; 5:6-21). In the last century a similar corvée of Arab serfs built the Suez canal near where the Israelites served their bondage.

The city of Raamses had a more checkered history. At the time of the Hyksos conquest of Egypt this city was known as Tanis and was the capital out of which the Hyksos ruled Egypt; but that was back in Joseph's day. After the Hyksos were expelled from Egypt the city went to ruin, but Sethos I, the founder of the XIXth dynasty of Egypt, began the rebuilding of the site. His son Rameses

The Stele of Rameses II, the Pharaoh of the Exodus, showing the ruler before the god Amon-Re. *Photo courtesy the University Museum of the University of Pennsylvania, Philadelphia*

II, who was the Pharaoh of the Exodus, completed the city and embellished it until he made it a fit metropolis from which he planned to rule the world. He called it Raamses. This Pharaoh anticipated Wendell Wilkie's "one world," but Rameses thought of it as one world subdued by Egypt's military power and absorbing Egypt's culture. He planned to make Africa and Asia one. Rameses had already willingly made himself half Semitic and worshiped the gods of the Canaanites as well as those of the Egyptian pantheon. But while Pharaoh was planning to reshape the world into an Egyptian empire, God was already busy at a greater task, i.e., creating Israel, a nation unique in all the world's history.

When we speak of Moses as history's most unique statesman we must remember that we are emphasizing *God's work in Moses,* not Moses' work for God. Paul's phrase, "It is no longer I that live but Christ liveth in me," explains how it was that God made the statesman Moses. It was Moses' obedience to God which was the vital catalyst in this history. Israel was indeed only a tiny country; but down through the years the Christian Church has made Moses an international statesman on every mission field she has entered and that includes most of the world.

Today is one of the finest times in all of history for evaluating the statesman Moses, for the continents now throb with new governments both large and small, and every theory of state is under trial somewhere. We even have a new so-called Israel, although it is actually as far from the Mosaic Israel as east is from west.

Moses was God's choice, for the doctrine of providence is seen everywhere in the life of Moses. He was born an Israelite serf, but he was reared in Pharaoh's palace at Raamses. But when Moses took Egyptian law into his own

The Springs of Moses near Mt. Nebo. © *Matson Photo Service*

hands in order to help his fellow Israelites he was forced to flee to Sinai to save his life. Thus Moses was equally at home in all matters Israelite and Egyptian; and in addition he was disciplined by the desert and coached by his Midianite father-in-law. The Midianites were a small nation which dominated much of Sinai as well as similar terrain east of the Gulf of Aqabah. Their skill as international traders and coppermen made them important far beyond their geographic size.

Mt. Sinai witnessed the two most climactic experiences in the life of Moses. As a refugee he met God here in the burning bush and received the impossible command to free the Israelite people from Egyptian bondage. Here he later received the Ten Commandments, which likewise were impossible orders, but in addition these were for all mankind and for all eternity! Here at Mt. Sinai God revealed Himself as Yahweh, whose name and nature mean "He who causes to be what comes into existence."

Here in Yahweh is Someone absolutely unique in the history of religion! Before Moses there had been a few tenuous *approaches* to monotheism but they always ended in a dead-end street and returned to a common paganism. The so-called monotheism of Akhenaten of Egypt is the best known of these "approaches" to monotheism. It was actually nothing but a mathematical monotheism, for it simply denied deity to all gods except one and attributed all the work of all the other deities to this "one" god. You will soon lose interest in such an approach to monotheism when you discover that it permitted Pharaoh Akhenaten to marry his own daughter!

Only Israel had a true monotheism and that was a revealed monotheism, not a rationalized one. The God who revealed Himself to Moses was omnipresent. He was without locale. No earthly site could ever localize Him and when the Israelites of Jeremiah's day tried to chain Him down to a Jerusalem temple, God destroyed both nation and temple. (It remained for the Byzantine Church to make Mt. Sinai a shrine.) God was the Creator of the world and was equally at home inside or outside of it.

God also refused to accept any visible representation of Himself, either idol or other symbol. One of the ways by which the archaeologist can follow Joshua's conquest in Palestine is by the little household Astartes (i.e., figures of the sex goddess) and other Canaanite symbols found in the cities Joshua destroyed. In striking contrast the succeeding Israelite cities show an absence of these same idols. The early Israelites were aniconic with a vengeance and destroyed all Canaanite idols.

Another unique characteristic of Yahweh was that He was neither "god nor goddess." Deity now was infinitely beyond gender i.e., beyond anything human. The true relation between deity and humanity was not revealed until the coming of Christ. On the other hand, the Old Testament is alive with use of anthropomorphic phraseology for Yahweh. Yet never does Yahweh become human. In the Old Testament God is at the same time closer than breathing but also more distant than east and west. And God is *holy* — not only sinless but also the Saviour of sinners.

One striking feature of Yahweh's dealing with men in crises periods was the use of miracles. Miracles are rare in Scripture. In the Old Testament they are concentrated about the names Moses, Elijah and Elisha. These were the times of faithless people — Israelites by name but not by nature. But the God of *grace* in both the Old Testament and the New Testament was ever ready to create even new natural phenomena i.e., miracles, to win back His wayward children. Science can never double check these miracles of God. They are seen and understood by faith alone. But Israel's history and the Church's history are absolutely unintelligible unless one accepts the miracle-working God and His miracle-working Christ.

Look now at the dramatic setting of the miracle of the Passover. It is preceded by the last of the plagues, the death of the first-born. To appreciate this plague we must remember that every Pharaoh was an incarnation of the Egyptian sun god, the supreme deity in all of Egypt. Therefore when Pharaoh Rameses II would die, his son would be the next incarnation of the sun god. If one may use the language of the boxing-ring, the plagues were a ten-round bout to see whether Yahweh was god or whether Pharaoh was god. But Pharaoh's first-born, i.e. the next sun god died, and Yahweh's deity was demonstrated to all. The earlier plagues also each dealt with a lesser god of Egypt or Palestine. Thus ten times Pharaoh challenged Yahweh with one of his own deities and each time he lost.

Now God ordered the Passover and demanded the observance of every minutia of the ritual. Any negligent Israelite was treated as any pagan Egyptian. God had no double standards of morals. Obedience and death were the crucial features in the test of Abraham and Isaac; and it was the same with Moses and the Israelites. This Passover is the blood atonement prophetic of the Lamb of God whose blood is on the door of heaven. Time is rarely emphasized in Scripture, so it is very significant that the Passover marks the beginning of a new calendar — a yearly calendar with Passover as New Year's day. Up to this time the only religious holiday was the Sabbath. With the resurrection of Christ, notice that the old weekly calendar of creation was restored, for the new creation uses the old calendar of the first creation. The New Testament has no yearly calendar. That was a later invention of the church.

The next major legal action on God's part was the giving of the Ten Commandments (Exodus 19ff). These Ten Commandments are absolutely unique among ancient law codes. They are still binding on the believer for Christ exemplified them and denied any basic retraction. Although the Ten Commandments are God's specific orders, nevertheless God insisted that they be ratified by Israel and they were voluntarily ratified three times — Exodus 19:8; 24:3,7. The Ten Commandments are expanded in Exodus, Leviticus, Numbers and Deuteronomy into a common civil and religious code dealing with the major and minor crimes and sins of that day.

The Mosaic date of this legislation is demonstrated by the absence of laws dealing with the industrial revolution of the days which came at the time of the written prophets. The Mosaic code was an excellent workable law for an agricultural civilization but it did not anticipate the problems of the industrial revolution of Isaiah's day. The kings Hezekiah and Josiah and all the prophets put together never produced a workable code for the industrial revolution of their day. There was no second Moses.

These legal codes of the Exodus period were for both church and state. Note that the same Passover law applied to Israelite and stranger alike. Following out this same policy, when Saul was made king, he was compelled to keep the Mosaic law exactly the same as any other Israelite. Likewise even the high priest had to make a sin offering before Yahweh.

American legal codes are rooted in the Mosaic code

and modified by the New Testament. Unfortunately they are also modified by concepts that are anti-Bible. Our democracy is not based on Greece but on Israel. This is especially true of our federal government. Unfortunately both ancient Israel and the modern U.S.A. have too often placed human wisdom above the divine. Too often have believers everywhere called Him *Saviour* but at the same time have refused to obey Him as *Lord*.

The tabernacle and the objects that went with its worship show Egyptian roots but its Sinai mutations were of God and it was these mutations that made its worship unique, for they were predictive of the New Testament dispensation. The tabernacle was a modified form of a miniature, mobile Egyptian temple. One such is portrayed on an Egyptian temple wall where Egyptian priests are shown praying for Rameses II, the Pharaoh of the Exodus, in his great decisive battle with the Hittites for world empire. This is the kind of a temple which God remodeled for His own worship in the desert wanderings of Israel.

Moses died in Trans-Jordan. He like other Israelites had taken obedience too lightly on a crucial occasion. No tombstone pays him homage but Deuteronomy says of him, "And there hath not arisen a prophet since in Israel like unto Moses, whom Yahweh knew face to face" (Deuteronomy 34:10).

Let us quickly summarize the work of Moses as a statesman. He was an Israelite of the Israelites and yet he was trained in Pharaoh's palace. Thus he was blessed with an Israelite faith and patriotism; but since he was reared in Pharaoh's palace he could at the same time appreciate and use all that was good in Egyptian culture. Furthermore since Palestine was an integral part of the

The famous statue of Moses by Michelangelo. *Radio Times
Hulton Picture Library, British Broadcasting Company, London*

Egyptian empire Moses was also familiar with all the political, legal and religious phases of Palestinian life.

But more important than this human training was his personal relationship with God; and it was his work as God's agent that made Moses the unique statesman. First, he led a people out of serfdom to the world's greatest empire and welded them into a nation which endured for approximately 1300 years. Second, that nation was directly responsible to God. Moses was only God's agent. Thus the world witnessed a God-designed nation, not a humanly fashioned one. The condensed fundamental law code was the Ten Commandments where man's duties are first to God and then to his fellow man. These Ten Commandments were and still are unique. They are to be obeyed simply because God so orders it. This basic law code of Sinai, however, was not thrust upon Israel. They were allowed to accept or reject it and three times this choice was presented to them. Thus in one sense Israel was a democracy for she chose her own law code. But more important she was a theocracy for that choice was *given* her by God and the nation was responsible to Him rather than to herself. Israel's forty years in the desert was the punishment for her disobeying God; and Moses himself was not permitted to enter the promised land because of his sin.

The Ten Commandments were expanded into a very detailed set of laws dealing with both civil and religious life. The civil law was basically God's modification of common Semitic law. Early American law was a modification of English common law. But it was not God's modification of English law. Although much of the sacrificial law looked like Semitic common sacrificial practice it was unique in its meaning. Remember that what is symbolized is more important than the symbol. The government is infinitely more important than the flag that symbolizes it. Thus the Israelite sacrificial system disappears in the New Testament but only because its meaning is intensified, illuminated and vitalized by the sacrificial death of Jesus Christ.

Under Moses Israel was a nation powerless apart from God. Yahweh and He alone brought Israel out of Egypt. He alone sustained them in the forty years of wilderness travel and He conquered Palestine for them. These miracles all Israelite historians and theologians and poets admitted. Moses was the mediator between God and man; and time and again he pleaded for God's mercy on a wayward and an unthankful people. This is the final qualification of a true statesman.

Now compare the founders of all the new states created in our lifetime with Moses, and they stand out only by way of contrast. Over the whole sweep of history Moses holds up equally well for his legal code covered both church and state; and they see improvement only in the New Testament when the Holy Spirit Himself takes His place in the heart of the believer.

But when we put the Mosaic law up against modern legal codes we must also remember its historic background. The Mosaic code must always be set over against the religious codes of its environment, i.e. the faiths of Egypt and Canaan. After one has plowed through the so-called religions of those two countries and then rereads the Mosaic code, it is like passing from death into life. History knows *no* religion *so* depraved as that of Canaan. Just recall the story of Sodom and Gomorrah and compare it with the Ten Commandments.

The best evaluations of Moses, however, are witnessed when Christ shares His transfiguration with Moses and when the redeemed in Revelation 15:3 sing the song of Moses and the song of the Lamb. Study also Luke 16:29-31 and Hebrews 3:1-2.

*   *   *   *

For archaeological data on Moses, see W. F. Albright *From the Stone Age to Christianity*, pp. 257-272 and *The Biblical Period from Abraham to Ezra*, Chapter II; also M. G. Kyle *Moses and the Monuments*.

Joshua, Whose Name Means Jesus

CHAPTER III

Joshua, Whose Name Means Jesus

A copper spearhead. *Kelso*

The Hebrew name of Moses' successor is hard to pro-
nounce in both English and Greek, so the name is brought
across as Joshua in our Old Testament and as Jesus in
our New Testament. Its original meaning signifies that
"Yahweh saves." But since most Christians are normally
a selfish people we think only of the saving work of Jesus

— forgetting that Jesus, as the judge of all men, must mete out death as well as life.

Six hundred years before Joshua's invasion God had told Abraham that the iniquity of the Amorite was not yet full (Genesis 15:16). But at the same time God destroyed Sodom and Gomorrah as a token pledge of what Palestine would receive if she continued on in sin. After this six centuries of probation Canaan did not repent of her sins and so Joshua must be God's agent enforcing the death sentence. But note that those who asked for mercy received it, as did Rahab's family and the city of Gibeon. Joshua was an agent of both damnation and of grace — a true forerunner of his namesake Jesus.

When the book of Joshua is opened the archaeologist finds that it is illustrated by a wealth of new material from the excavations made on the sites of seven of the cities captured by Joshua. Most of the seven have demonstrated that the destruction of these cities by the Israelites was cataclysmic — an annihilation of things Canaanite. On the other hand such cities as Beth-shean and Megiddo, which are specifically mentioned as not captured, have been dug up and these show a continuing Canaanite occupation exactly the opposite of what we find in those cities captured by Joshua. This mass of material from so many different cities in various sections of Palestine makes an ideal demonstration of the accuracy of the Bible narrative.

Joshua apparently had served in the Egyptian army, for Moses used him as the military leader in the Sinai wilderness and Trans-Jordan. Foreigners were common in the Egyptian army. One of the later Pharaohs had actually been a foreigner in the Egyptian military service. The earlier campaigns in Sinai and Trans-Jordan where Joshua served as commander under Moses, have not yet been enlightened by excavations. We can follow Joshua the moment he crosses over into west Palestine. Unfortunately the archaeologist cannot throw much light on the capture of Jericho. That city was built of mud-dried bricks, and as soon as the city was laid waste those bricks simply dissolved back into mud under every rain. When this mud dried into dust, it was then blown away by the strong winds of the Jordan valley. Even greater erosions than those of Joshua's date are seen in the earlier history of Jericho, whose foundation goes back to about 7500 B.C. by carbon 14 dating, thus making it the oldest city in the world.

Père Vincent, who was the best Palestinian archaeologist at the time the Germans excavated Jericho before World War I, saw typical pottery of the conquest period at Jericho. The German surveyors, however, were unable to discover any exact house plans of that Canaanite period. In later digs, Miss Kenyon was able to locate one room and some tombs of the conquest period. There is only one clue left by which we could determine the size of the city and that would be to locate and excavate the Canaanite cemetery, but this would be a very expensive procedure.

Other excavations on the sites of these conquered cities demonstrate the catastrophic destruction wrought by Joshua's troops. I have personally dug in the thick ash-loaded debris left by Joshua's conquest at Bethel and at Kiriath-sepher. These were the worst destructions found in the many levels dug at both cities. The Late Bronze Canaanite cities at Bethel represented some of the finest domestic construction of that period in all of Palestine, but the Israelites destroyed these houses completely. In contrast to these excellent Canaanite buildings, the houses built by Joshua's troops were nothing but hovels. These

Revetment of the city wall of Kiriath-sepher, captured by Joshua's troops. The perpendicular section of the wall originally rose about 20 feet above this revetment. *Kelso*

troops were desert born and had always lived in tents. When they tried to build stone houses, they were unable to construct high solid walls of field stone as did the Canaanites. Indeed, the Israelites had to intersperse piers made of large stones piled on top of one another to hold up the roof beams. The Israelite doorways were so low that even a short person had to bend over in order to enter a house. The ashes of the Canaanite destruction in both

Bethel and Kiriath-sepher were deeper than the debris of any other destruction found on these sites. At times the Canaanite debris was about a yard deep. Much of this was ashes from the grain that had been stored in the houses. This depth of ashes demonstrates the terrific conflagration that destroyed these cities. Some of the sun-dried bricks were actually baked as hard as kiln bricks.

There must have been bumper crops during the years preceding the conquest to give so much ash. These bumper crops are also demonstrated by the fact that Moses had been able to detour far out into the desert so as to by-pass Edom and Moab. This is possible only when the major rain cycles move east of their normal course and thus make the desert blossom as the rose. This section of the Trans-Jordan desert is good soil but lacks sufficient normal rainfall for farming under the normal cyclonic circle.

Joshua's military policy was a blend of surprise and speed. The former is seen in his attack on Jericho, which was conducted at the height of the flood season of the Jordan when the melting snow and the late winter rains sometimes make the river a mile wide. The defenders of Jericho naturally assumed that no attack could be made at such high flood stage.

Surprise and speed were also blended in Joshua's Ajalon campaign when his troops marched from Jericho to Gibeon overnight. Only a desert-trained army could have done this impossible task. That surprise maneuver put Joshua on the high rim of the Ajalon canyon at Gibeon from which he could sweep down the canyon and destroy his Canaanite enemies who were wearily trudging up that steep pass. Furthermore God came to Joshua's assistance with a terrific hail storm, with the result that the enemy

The famous "Israel Tablet" of Pharaoh Merneptah at Thebes, mentioning the arrival of the Israelites in Palestine. *Photo courtesy Cairo Museum (Egyptian National Museum, Cairo, Egypt)*

suffered a greater loss from this storm than from the Israelite troops. The destructive nature of hail is seen in a storm
at Moradad, India, May 1st, 1888, which cost 250 lives.
Arabia only a few years ago had a similar storm where
the hail came down as sheets of ice. The American record
of hail is 17 inches in circumference with a weight of one
and one-half pounds.

The Canaanites retreated down the canyon but Joshua
destroyed most of their army before it could reach the
fortified cities of the Shephelah. Joshua then quickly
stormed these fortresses whose defenders were now only a
skeleton force of the very young and the very old, for the
men of military age had gone into the Ajalon fray. After
the completion of the conquest of the fortresses in the
Shephelah Joshua climbed the hill road to Hebron, the
natural capital of the Judaean plateau and thus he completed the encirclement of southern Palestine. The Egyptian Pharaoh, Merneptah, in an inscription dated in 1232
B.C. mentions this Israelite campaign but plays down its
importance.

The crossing of the Jordan at high flood and the cyclonic hail storm at Ajalon are of special theological significance, for Baal was the great Canaanite storm god who
was supposed to control the rain, the hail, the snow and
the floods of Palestine. These episodes proved that Baal
was as powerless before Yahweh in Palestine as he had
been in the episode of the plagues of Egypt. The Israelites
always frankly admitted the major part which God's providence had played in the conquest. Here are the words of
the Psalmist. "We have heard with our ears, O God, our
fathers have told us, What work thou didst in their days,
In the day of old. For they gat not the land in possession
by their own sword, Neither did their own arm save them;

But thy right hand, and thine arm, and the light of thy countenance, Because thou wast favorable unto them" (Psalm 44:1,3). Joshua himself in renewing the covenant at Shechem had frankly told the Israelites that they did not win the war with sword or bow, cf. Joshua 24:12. Israel was always glad to give God the credit for the conquest of Palestine, even though their army had played its part well.

Joshua did not need to take military action against Shechem for the inhabitants of the area voluntarily joined Joshua. Neither the Bible nor archaeology throw any positive light on this merger. A few clues in the Old Testament seem to suggest that when Israel went to Egypt some representatives were left behind to hold title to the Palestine real estate. Also during their Egyptian sojourn other Israelites seem to have returned to Palestine. Furthermore, relatives from Padan-Aram may well have settled here later. But whatever may be the merger story it is highly significant that Shechem is the place where the Israelites renewed the Sinai covenant, as Moses had commanded.

Shechem was often in the headlines of Israel's history. It was the first city mentioned in the Abraham narrative as he enters Palestine. Jacob's sons massacred the native population of Shechem. Joshua renewed the Sinai covenant here and Abimelech, a son of Gideon, started an abortive monarchy here. This was where Jeroboam I founded the northern kingdom of Israel. The Samaritans made this their religious center after Alexander the Great captured Samaria. The Samaritan temple here was destroyed by the Maccabees and Jesus talked with the woman of Samaria at Jacob's well just outside Shechem. Even today Nablus, the modern successor of Shechem, is often in the headlines of the newspapers of the kingdom of Jordan.

And its history is still as erratic as was that of ancient Shechem.

The Bible text tells us that Joshua did not destroy some of the key fortresses such as Megiddo and Beth-shean of the Esdraelon pass to the Jordan, but he did annihilate the city of Hazor which dominated all of Galilee. Megiddo and Beth-shean are both important to the study of the conquest period and the judges for they were originally key Egyptian fortresses in Palestine. Statues and inscriptions from the Pharaohs have been found in their excavations. These cities also illustrate the continuing prosperous Canaanite culture and its immoral religions in those Palestinian cities which were not captured by Joshua. Such cities became tragic troublemakers for Israel in the days of the judges i.e., "the struggle period" when Israel was debating whether to remain loyal to Yahweh or to back-slide into Canaanite paganism.

Hazor was by far Joshua's greatest military victory for Hazor was the largest and the wealthiest city in all of Palestine. It was over a hundred times larger than Megiddo. In comparison with Hazor, Jericho was simply a minor border fortress. How Joshua was able to capture Hazor is still unknown; no miraculous assistance is mentioned as at Jericho or Ajalon. In evaluating the capture of Hazor one must also remember that Joshua had a desert army untrained in siege operations. Hazor was originally the greatest Hyksos city in Palestine. Its massive walls of beaten earth were erected by these conquerors from the land beyond the Caspian Sea to protect their horses and chariots which were the secret of their great military power. Although erected before 1700 B.C. these massive earthworks still look as if they were a part of the original terrain.

Palestine is a geographer's paradise because of the vast variety of terrain in so small an area. But that diversity only complicated the military problems which a general must solve. Any modern military man who has traveled over the super complicated terrain of Palestine pays high tribute to Joshua, and would be glad to have such a general in active service today. Stonewall Jackson and Patton would have enjoyed working with Joshua. Allenby was glad to learn from Joshua.

But Joshua was much more than a military man. He had been understudy to Moses in the wilderness and God chose him as Moses' successor. Like Moses he was Israel's civil leader and the maker of her religious policy. Note the parallels in Joshua's life to those of Moses. Joshua like Moses was granted a theophany (Joshua 5:13-15). He led Israel dryshod over Jordan as Moses had done over the Red Sea. He reinstituted the law at Mts. Gerizim and Ebal as Moses had reinstituted it in Moab. Also God hardened the hearts of the Canaanites for Joshua as he had hardened the heart of Pharaoh for Moses (Joshua 11:20).

Joshua was as much of a religious leader as a military one. He governed Israel by the supernatural law of Sinai. The Ark preceded his army over Jordan, and Jericho was primarily a church victory. Here also Joshua reinstituted circumcision. War waited on worship at Shechem; and any Canaanite who asked mercy was spared — witness Rahab's family and the Gibeonites. Joshua also renewed the covenant of his nation at Shechem a second time, i.e. just before his death as Moses had done in Moab.

Equally as important as Joshua's military conquest (although this is seldom stressed) was his division of the land. He was one of those rare military geniuses who is

Excavating the old city wall of ancient Jericho. The Mt. of
Temptation is in the background. © *Matson Photo Service*

equally as successful in the days of peace as in the days of war. Although some of Joshua's tribal allotments changed their boundaries at various times and some cities were credited to different tribes at different times, nevertheless the all-over geographic picture remained relatively stationary throughout the nation's history. This is a magnificent tribute to the geographic judgment of Joshua. He had been key man among the spies sent out by Moses; and this experience plus his military campaigns fitted him for this work. A general must be a good geographer. But Joshua was more. He put each of these various conquering tribes upon a natural geographic area and thus prevented civil wars which so often follow similar military conquests. But remember that the actual distribution of the land to the various tribes was by casting lots. God, not Joshua, said "what tribe went where."

Joshua's military campaign had centered on the key fortresses. But in any mountain country such as Palestine the mopping up process is still a difficult and time-consuming task. Joshua ordered this consolidation of the land to be done by the individual tribes. Let each master his own lot; he would then appreciate his land!

On the question of creating permanent geographic boundaries Joshua has had few rivals in the history of small countries. Today Europe, Asia and Africa could well study his use of terrain and ecology in laying out their major and minor national boundaries. But now, as then, good boundaries are of little value unless God distributes the land and the people obey Him!

*   *   *   *

For archaeological data on Joshua, see W. F. Albright, *The Biblical Period from Abraham to Ezra,* Chapter III.

The Israelite Judgeships and the
New Nations of Today

CHAPTER IV

The Israelite Judgeships and the New Nations of Today

A fertility goddess

The Bible student of today is better able to sympathize with the Israelites of the days of the Judges, since we see how few of the new nations of today are able to handle their problems any better.

Israel had no leader of major caliber to succeed Joshua; and so with his death all the unresolved problems of the nation suddenly exploded at once. One of the secrets of Joshua's success was that Israel was a solid unit fighting against the Canaanites who were divided into petty states. But as soon as each Israelite tribe settled within its own boundaries selfishness now dominated their policy; and this jeopardized the national unity which had made the conquest possible. There were even periods of civil war, and the tribe of Benjamin was almost exterminated. Meanwhile the various Canaanite groups still left in the land united against the isolated tribes. Thus the period of the Judges is to a large degree a period of Israel's distress — strikingly in contrast with the preceding days of Joshua and the succeeding days of David.

The Bible outlines the period of the Judges in five phases.

1. There arose a generation after Joshua who knew Yahweh not by experience but by hearsay. Judges 2:10.

2. They forsook Yahweh and served the Baalim. Judges 2:11-12.

3. God delivered them into the hands of the spoilers who despoiled them. Judges 2:14; 3:8; 6:1.

4. Then Israel cried unto God for help. Judges 6:6; 10:10.

5. Yahweh raised up judges who saved them. Judges 2:16; 3:9, 15.

The vicious circle returned again and again (Judges 2:19). In theory God was Israel's supreme ruler to whom absolute obedience had been pledged at Sinai and renewed at Shechem. But in practice "every man did that which was right in his own eyes" (Judges 21:25).

During most of this period Israel had no single judge over all the land. Usually a few tribes banded together

Left: The house in which the men are working was built in the days of Joshua. The large, tall stone behind the workmen was originally a sacred pillar from a Canaanite high place. The paved floor in the foreground is from a house about the time of Isaiah. *Kelso*

Bottom: The lower well referred to in Judges 1:15 ("Spring" is an incorrect translation). Shepherds are watering their flocks while singing "The Song of the Well." *Kelso*

in an emergency alliance. Sometimes these were in Trans-Jordan, sometimes in Galilee, sometimes in southern Cis-Jordan. The Israelites' troubles were also compounded by the fact that most of them had to learn the art of farming for the first time from the conquered Canaanites. (In the desert only rare spots of land can be tilled.) To the Canaanites farming and religion were inseparable; so to them farming demanded the worship of their fertility gods and goddesses with an active participation in sexual orgies at their high places. Too many Israelite farmers took their Canaanite agricultural advisors seriously and abandoned Yahweh for Baal. It was the old story, "You cannot serve God and mammon." Canaanite religion was the most depraved of all the religions known to scholarship. Intellectually it was crude and degenerate. Magic and divination mingled with child sacrifice and orgiastic worship. This is the religion which fought its life and death struggle with Israel.

One word of caution, however, is wise in evaluating the epoch of the Judges. In the Pentateuch we have the ideals of godly living and their expression in the legal codes, whereas in the book of Judges we have the "police blotter." Throughout all of history the books in the lawyer's office and the records in the police court have usually been at high variance. Nevertheless it was the sudden and widespread abandonment of God after all the unique blessings they received under Moses and Joshua that made Israel's sin so heinous.

The art of war received a new contribution in this period. The Midianites introduced the camel into military action (Judges 6:5; 7:12) and with it they revolutionized Palestinian warfare, especially in Trans-Jordan. (The Hyksos had earlier revolutionized warfare by introduction

of the horse-drawn spoked chariot.) When the Israelites
came through that area under Moses, three tribes had asked
to be settled there. It was then a very safe territory, for
the desert was a sure defense on the east and the Jordan
chasm protected it on the west. Thus only Manasseh on
the north and Reuben on the south had a foreign boundary.

The camel changed all that. The desert tribes could
now use the Wadi Sirhan to the east as a major base of
supplies and from it could suddenly raid any of the three
Israelite tribes. There was no easy defense against these
lightning invasions. Indeed, the Ammonites soon became
the major camel power in Trans-Jordan and remained so
up to the destruction of Jerusalem by Nebuchadnezzar.
They also cashed in on the camel as the burden-bearer for
commerce. The donkey was now replaced by the camel except for farm work and local travel. The camel can carry
approximately 500 pounds on good terrain. He lives on
the poorest of desert vegetation and can go long distances
without water.

With the Samson story we concentrate on the Philistines who came into Palestine somewhere about 1175 B.C.
They introduced a new military weapon. They brought
the long slashing sword to the battlefield to defeat the
short stabbing sword commonly used at that time. The
Philistines also introduced the new metal, iron, into the
arts of both war and peace. When they forged the steel
sword they had a weapon much superior to Israel's bronze
sword.

Furthermore the Philistines, like the Israelites, were
a homeless people and the only available country for their
settlement was Palestine. They had been driven out of
their homes in Anatolia and fled south. They had invaded

Egypt hoping to settle there but they were repulsed and had to fall back upon the coastal plain of Palestine. This happened shortly after Joshua's death. Thus Palestine became a battleground to the death in which Israelite or Philistine had to be annihilated for neither people could return to Egypt. The fortunes of this war to the death swayed back and forth before David finally made Israel not only the master of Palestine, but also practically all the land between modern Turkey and Egypt. The Philistines, however, won one major victory. They left their name indelibly imprinted on the land for we know it as Palestine.

Another military exploit to be noted was Abimelech's seizure of power at Shechem. Here was an attempt to introduce a full-blown Canaanite dictatorship; and it was made by a son of Gideon one of the most loyal of the Israelite Judges. The revolt, however, was a failure.

Most of the space of the book of Judges is given over to those rulers who were military saviours of the nation but one third of the men mentioned as judges were not from the military. They were essentially men of peace and their prestige seems to have been in their ability to arbitrate tribal differences and thus prevent fighting. This emphasis on the prestige of the civilian as a peacemaker, even if it does occupy only a small part of the book, is one of the high points of this political period. The civil judge and the military general were both God's agents in shaping Israel's history.

In comparison with Moses and Joshua the judges were little men. They lacked the stalwart spiritual faith of Moses and Joshua and they had little genius for government. In plain English they did not live close enough to God. Many a critic of the book would make these men worse than they were; but the Bible gives them the title of judge and saviour (Judges 2:16,18; 3:9,15). Notice the political background of these men. They were first chosen by God and then his choice was confirmed by the people. This is the same method that God used with Moses and Joshua and would use again with Saul and David. If the judges were little men; and they were little men; nevertheless God was using the best talent available and disciplining both judge and people by his providential workings of history, that all might grow in stature and favor with God and man.

The book closes with an epigram which is descriptive not only of the period of the Judges but of most of the world's history from the days of Adam up to the present. "Every man did what was right in his own eyes." All too seldom does any leader great or small, or any nation strong or weak cry out, "My Lord and my God," and then obey Him.

By way of fair play, the book of Judges should be compared with the emergent nations of today, especially since the latter have about 3000 years advantage. There may be less warfare now, but otherwise the chaotic conditions of almost every phase of these new emergent nations' life is all too similar to the Israel of the Judges. Alas, this book of the Judges has too often been the pattern used for the shaping of much of human history. Even Europe and America are now passing through such a phase. The Church today is calling Christ *Saviour*, but refusing to follow Him as *Lord*.

Sex is often as dominant now as Baal and Astarte were then, though of course, we are too sophisticated to give it ecclesiastical standing. The prohibition amendment to the constitution was the greatest moral victory in human history brought about without years of bloodshed; but the Church helped to take it off the law book. Today we are such a drunken nation that even big business and government policy must adjust itself to the drunkard. It is estimated that gamblers in America spend two hundred and fifty times as much money on gambling as the church spends for foreign missions. Even dogs and cats fare better in the American pocketbook than God, because foreign missions (the heart of Christianity) receive only one-twentieth of what the dogs and cats get.

There is one good piece of political news out of the period of the Judges that does deserve high credit. The Bible narrative on how the judges were chosen is not the only feature that demonstrates democracy in Israel. The archaeologist has discovered that the Israelite houses and their contents demonstrate that Israel was an incipient democracy. Practically all Israelite houses in this period were similar — all of a common pattern. The poverty of their contents was also similar. This is in striking contrast to the Canaanite houses which were destroyed by Joshua. There the houses of the rich and poor were in startling contrast. To be sure the Israelites were poor, but they were equals. Democracy was to be the Church's gift to political science.

*   *   *   *

For additional archaeological data see W. F. Albright *The Biblical Period from Abraham to Ezra,* Chapter IV.

The Statesmen David and Churchill

Chapter V

The Statesmen David and Churchill

A javelin head

When Winston Churchill died, Great Britain laid to rest one of the greatest figures in all of her long history — a man at home in war and peace, a statesman, an artist and a champion of the uniqueness of his people. Now if you will compare Churchill with David you will discover that they had much in common and that the two worlds in which they lived were much the same in essence, although the externalities may seem quite different.

Before we can place the two giants side by side for comparison, we must highly condense much of the crucially important data of I Samuel. The book opens with Samuel, the last of the judges and the first of the prophets. He was by far the most versatile of the judges. His legal ability put him on the circuit judgeship and he served as a military leader before Saul. Since he had been adopted by Eli he became a Levite and refused Saul any part in the sacrificial service. At God's command he anointed both Saul and David. Samuel was the nation's one stabilizing factor in the reign of Saul. The New Testament credits him as the first of the prophets; and he is the first to make new, joint political-religious moves — adjusting the new national problem of a king to the spirit of the Mosaic law. Note also that with the loss of the tabernacle the Israelite priesthood declined in influence until after the dedication of Solomon's temple. Meanwhile laymen were taking a greater place in the Church. David, for example, added music to the church service and the prophets began their influential work in trying to reform both church and state.

Another major historical factor was the destruction of Shiloh and its tabernacle. In this action the Philistines destroyed the one and only important federal feature that was left in Israel during the Judges. Shiloh was the one shrine sacred to each and all of the twelve tribes. Here the Aaronic priesthood presided over the entire nation's sacrificial ritual. Here alone was God's meeting place with Israel as a unit. The Philistines reasoned that with Israel's central sanctuary destroyed that the nation would collapse and its people could be integrated with the Philistine population.

The Israelites responded to this religious loss with a pagan request for a king "like the nations round about them." The word king is not important here for it is just a synonym for judge. "Then all the elders of Israel gathered themselves together, and came to Samuel unto Ramah; and they said unto him, Behold, thou art old, and thy sons walk not in thy ways: now make us a *king* to *judge* us like all the nations" (I Samuel 8:4-5). What the Israelites really asked for was a *military dictatorship like the Philistines.* Samuel recognized this as a repudiation of Yahweh, but nevertheless he presented their plea to God, although at the same time pointing out to them that their request was a denial of the government policy introduced by Moses and still intact (though little enforced). The new federal government which the Israelites requested is succinctly summarized by Samuel (I Samuel 8:11-17). Under that policy there would now be a *federal* army drafted by the king, provisioned by him and supplied with arms by him. The original military policy and the one still in use was a *national guard in each tribe responsible to that tribe alone.* All twelve tribes could unite under a common leader as Joshua, or only a few tribes could acknowledge a common commander as Jephthah. Each soldier provided his own food and weapons. Now the king would draft an army. And the king would appoint whatever officers he desired even to the lowest ratings. The king would need to confiscate enough farm land to supply his commissary. Furthermore he must reward his best officers with farms, which again he must confiscate from the common man. He would need to build national armories to manufacture the weapons for his soldiers.

For international prestige Israel's king would need to have a palace with luxury equal to that of the Philistines, and that would mean drafting both men and women to staff his palace complex. Furthermore Israel would have to pay a second tithe. God would still get the original tithe, but the king would demand a second tithe to be paid in grain and flocks! But terror destroyed sanity and they pressed for a king "like the nations round about them." God denied their request for an absolute monarch but granted them instead a "constitutional monarch" (I Samuel 8:22; 12:13-25). God preserves His prerogative of choosing a leader, for Saul is chosen by Him (9:15-17) and anointed by His agent (10:1). The people publicly accepted God's choice of a king (10:20-24) just as they accepted His choice of Moses, Joshua and the Judges. Saul was officially made king before Yahweh in Gilgal after his first victory. God modified the Mosaic code by an amendment on the office of a king which, like the law, was laid up "before Yahweh" (10:25). This amendment demanded that king and people alike must obey God (12:13-25).

The army used this amendment, for they refused to let Saul kill Jonathan, who had unwittingly broken an edict of his father Saul. Neither would the army obey Saul's orders to kill the priests at Nob. As a military leader Saul restored Trans-Jordan to Israelite domination but it was touch and go with the Philistines west of Jordan. He lost the battle of Gilboa and that gave the Philistines the Jordan valley and all the land between it and the Mediterranean coast. As a statesman Saul was a total failure. The best we could call him today would be a poor politician. As a spiritual leader he was still worse.

Now to return to David and his rise in power. Although chosen early in Saul's reign by God and anointed by Samuel as king, he refused to think of reigning while Yahweh's other anointed (Saul) was living. He genuinely lamented the death of Yahweh's anointed. After Saul's death David made no political move until after he had prayed God as to whether or not he should take over the kingship (II Samuel 2:1). David was first made king over Judah only. When he was chosen king by all the tribes of Israel, it was in a covenant made before Yahweh (II Samuel 5:3). This was about 1000 B.C. David's revolt against the Philistine government called for a quick attack on David by the Philistines before David could consolidate his powers. But when the military campaign was over, the Philistines had disappeared from history as a military and a political power. There are later references to the Philistines in Scripture but these are to their old territory rather than to their nationality. Excavations at Ashdod, however, show that the Philistine religion still dominated that site through most of the Old Testament period.

The newly united Israelite nation needed a capital but ideally it should be one unrelated to either the northern or the southern tribes; so David captured Jerusalem. Joshua had conquered it but it had been lost to the Jebusites during the days of the Judges, probably early in that period just after the tribe of Benjamin had been almost annihilated. (Jerusalem had been allotted to Benjamin.) Thus Jerusalem was ideal neutral ground, a sort of Washington, D.C. To this political capital David brought the ark and planned to house it in a permanent temple. Saul had murdered most of the Aaronic priesthood and thus lost the allegiance of the spiritual citizens of the kingdom. David quickly salvaged what was left of the priestly line after the massacre and later restored it to the service of the tabernacle, which he erected in Jerusalem when denied the privilege of building the temple. Thus Jerusalem became the capital for both church and state but David kept them separate as they had been under Moses.

Now we are ready to compare David and Churchill. In the military field each found his nation in a desperate military tragedy; and each pulled his nation back into international power. David, however, was actual commander-in-chief in the field and extended the boundaries of his empire to the title-deed promised to Abraham, i.e. from the Euphrates to the Nile. For once, and once only Israel was the dominant world power in the Levant. David, however, would doubtless have been the first to admit that God's providential action in making Egypt and Assyria third rate powers was a major factor in Israel's victory. On the other hand Churchill was not a general in the field but as prime minister he did dictate the military policy for a British Commonwealth scattered around the world.

David's military conquests had a most unusual economic turn. His conquest of Syria made him one of the greatest, if not the greatest, "steel magnates" of his day. Iron was then coming into history as a new revolutionary metal which was quickly replacing copper. Its appearance, however, was not as sudden and as spectacular as that of aluminum in our own time. Israel profited so greatly from this versatile new metal coming out of Anatolia via Syria that the size of the plowshare which the farmer used was so increased that he could almost double the volume of his crops. This in turn in those days meant doubling the nation's population.

David and Churchill each had personality plus, and each was a natural leader. In statesmanship Churchill's problem was to preserve the English law and spirit. David

Top: Beth-shean, which was not captured by Joshua, but was destroyed by David. *Kelso*

Bottom: Ain Feshka as seen from the Qumran community. David led his flock to this same spring on the shore of the Dead Sea. *Kelso*

had a still greater problem, to reinstate the Mosaic law
and put vital life into it. Preserving faith in God is always
more difficult than preserving faith in one's nation. To
the ancient Israelites the Davidic kingdom was the climax
of their glory. He could have no superior except Messiah
Himself; and they called Messiah the Son of David.

David and Churchill both instinctively did the dramatic. Look at David in the Goliath episode. Read the
passage with this emphasis in mind. Note also the dramatic in the following: David's love for Jonathan, although Jonathan was heir apparent to Saul; David's
episodes with Saul at En-gedi and Ziph; his behavior
before Achish; etc., etc. But for drama nothing equals
David's lament at Absalom's death, unless it is his 51st
Psalm. Who ever heard of a king confessing in public
that he had broken the Ten Commandments and pleading
with God for mercy!

One major political sin, however, must be laid at
David's door — his numbering of the peoples (II Samuel
24). Interpreting these verses into a modern English idiom
we have the following: "David created a federal army,"
which was exactly what Samuel had feared that Saul would
do. Even the hardened sinner Joab, his commander in the
field, tried to dissuade David from this tragic step but he
failed. The nation likewise failed because it acquiesced
in this act. That is why the wrath of God is meted out
on everyone. When David said, "What have these sheep
done?" he was simply pleading for more mercy to them
than to himself, the initiator of the crime. But Israel was
not blameless. In Saul's day the people had used "their
referendum and recall" and had thus refused to allow
Saul to be an absolute dictator. David's people, however,
put their okay on his federal army.

David and Churchill were both artists. That term is here used in its basic sense of any person proficient in any one of the fine arts. Both men were geniuses with the pen, David in poetry, Churchill in prose. Each used the pen to exalt his beloved land and people, but David concentrated also on the God of Israel — his personal Good Shepherd.

In David's day songs were of a common authorship, that is the same man wrote the words and composed the music. Even in his youth David was so exceptional that he was called in to perform before King Saul; and a reading of the Psalms shows that David never laid down his harp nor stilled his voice. It used to be popular to deny David the Psalms attributed to him. But the archaeological research in Phoenicia and Qumran has given him back his copyrights.

The Syrians and the Palestinians were always known internationally as musicians. Even the Greeks learned from them. Many of the Psalms show Canaanite literary forms. Psalm 29 is a striking example of a converted Canaanite Psalm. The songs composed by the Essenes at Qumran are very different in style from the Old Testament Psalms. Furthermore, they are in large part a blending of quotations taken from Scripture. They also have a strong emphasis on mysticism.

Every phase of David's life bursts out into song. The shepherd world lives again. The temple service echoes and reechoes God's praise. Even war marches to his music. His songs mark both his victories and his defeats. There are songs of trust and desperate pleas for help. Both the vanity of life and the glories of life are his themes. The finest tribute to the Psalms is their use in connection with the death of Christ. As for ourselves we use his 23rd

Psalm in death and his 51st Psalm in life. The Psalter has always been the song book of the Christian church. Note that the New Testament did not write a new hymnal, although short hymns are scattered through its pages. We cannot overemphasize the fact that David introduced music as an integral part of the church service.

Although David did not write the fine prose that Churchill did, some of the best prose of the Old Testament dates from the days of David and Solomon. The narratives dealing with the lives of Samuel, Saul, David and Solomon are immortal prose. Sit down sometime and read these narratives through quickly, enjoying them as pure prose. Then reread them to get the timeless spiritual message that speaks to each succeeding generation. We are heavily indebted to the unknown literary men who told of David. They were excellent forerunners of Churchill's historic prose.

Churchill was also an artist with the brush but David could only paint word pictures. David, however, had as versatile a hand as Churchill, but his was the musician's hand. Even in his youth he was already playing before royalty but we know him best as one whose music was played before his God.

Both men were national heroes and will ever remain so. But to us David seems the greater, for his finest contributions were not to his nation but to the kingdom of God; and the melody of his music still echoes in every church. God said of him, "I have found David, the son of Jesse, a man after my own heart, who shall do all my will" (Acts 13:22). This is indeed a supreme tribute.

*   *   *   *

For additional archaeological data see W. F. Albright, *The Biblical Period from Abraham to Ezra,* Chapter V; and *Archaeology and the Religion of Israel,* pp. 119-129.

Solomon, the King With Many a Ph.D.

Chapter VI

Solomon, the King With Many a Ph.D.

A loom weight

Solomon's wisdom is best appreciated in the Near East, where today anything super-gigantic, distinctly unique, or unfathomably difficult is always attributed to Solomon or Alexander the Great. In the logic of the Near East, only these two geniuses could have done the impossible.

Solomon's wisdom was indeed versatile. To begin

with his less publicized scholarship, he was a botanist and a biologist (I Kings 4:33). In the former field he was at home with all plant life, from the tiny "hyssop that grows in the wall" to the greatest tree the ancients knew, the cedar of Lebanon. Palestine and Syria are said to have the greatest variety of flowers per square mile of any area on earth. Their flora reaches from the sub-tropics of the Dead Sea area (deepest spot on the globe) to the Lebanons over 10,000 feet high with its deep winter snow. When excavating New Testament Jericho, I commuted daily between Jerusalem and Jericho. The spring flowers along that road are simply impossible to describe, for variety, color and profusion. It seems impossible that God did invent so many varieties. The biologist, of course, had a parallel spread of animal life in those days, although many of these species have today been depleted. So much for Solomon, the scientist.

In the fine arts, Solomon specialized in two fields, literature and architecture. He should be entitled to degrees in both these fields. In the literary field his proverbs have been preserved in the book of that name. Among the Semites of antiquity and the Arabs of today, the proverb constitues a major form of literature. The proverb is a substantial truth, dramatically phrased, and condensed for quick and permanent memory, usually only two to four lines long. It was the child's school book, the phraseology of business and politics and the epigram by which you finally clinched your argument in court. The more subtle factors in the use of Proverbs is listed in the first six verses of the book. The English translation of Proverbs 1:7 is too thin. The play on words here is saying that the fear of Yahweh (i.e. obeying God) is the first thing and *always* the most important thing in knowledge (i.e. the experience of godly living). The book of Proverbs was Solomon's brochure on how to live the godly life. Its phraseology made it easier for the common man to understand and practice his faith. In its most common denominator, wisdom is godliness and foolishness is sin. The Pentateuch was the lawyer's book, but the common man kept out of the clutches of the law by practicing the precepts of Proverbs. The modern Arab says, "A proverb is to speech as salt is to food." So a Christian missionary in Arab countries must have a minimum of a thousand keen proverbs at the tip of his tongue for use on all occasions.

Solomon's interest in architecture was occasioned by the necessity of his building a central sanctuary in Jerusalem where all Israel could worship Yahweh. This temple was simply a modification of the mobile tabernacle of the Mosaic days put into a permanent stone sanctuary. The basic pattern of court, holy place and inner-sanctuary or most holy place remained. But the decorative features differed greatly. (God did not give specific plans and specifications to Solomon as He had to Moses.) A related ground plan is seen in the Syrian Temple of Tell Tainat. The Judaean city of Arad copied the Jerusalem pattern for its local sanctuary. Solomon's builders were Phoenicians and they apparently suggested most of the decorative changes.

These Phoenicians introduced into Palestine for the first time the structural wall which is built with headers and stretchers and uses quoin construction on the corners. They also introduced pilasters with proto-Aeolic capitals. They improved the quarrying and dressing of stone over any earlier Israelite work. The quarry which produced the stone for Solomon's temple can be seen in an enormous

Quarry from which stone for the Jerusalem Temple was taken.
© *Matson Photo Service*

cave underneath what is now the northern section of the Turkish walled city.

The Syrian custom of lining a temple with cedar panels was another new feature introduced into Solomon's temple. The use of the columns Jachin and Boaz in his temple was also a carry-over from Near East temple architecture. Their exact structural nature is disputed by scholars but these columns seem to have been used by Solomon to symbolize the pillars of cloud and fire that led the Israelites in their desert wanderings. Not only did Solomon double the size of the tabernacle when he erected his temple but he also surrounded it with a new structure with three floors of rooms on all sides of the temple except the front. These rooms were for the use of temple personnel and for the storage of materials used in the temple service. The new addition was built directly against the temple proper but not incorporated into its walls. The temple remained a completely separate and distinct unit as had been the tabernacle.

The wide use of copper and bronze in this temple should be noted. Hebrew has only the one word for both metals but the metallurgists of that day were so excellent that the use to which the metals were put tells us whether it was copper or one of the various tin alloys of copper. It was never brass, for that alloy was not discovered until centuries later. The Bible gives us details of this copper industry from the mines and smelters of the Arabah to Arabian markets via the port city of Ezion-geber. The skilled fashioning of the metal by hammering or casting, along with the cire perdue technique for the most delicate work was done in the Jordan valley near where the Jabbok River enters the Jordan. Read I Kings 7:13-59.

Solomon did not neglect his own royal buildings: palace, armory, throne room, etc. And, of course, his twelve new administrative capitals throughout the nation had to have their public buildings. Even his chariot depots used the clearstory in their stables.

One of the by-products of Solomon's temple-palace complex was a new type of house architecture among the common people. The government's prodigious demand for large drafted stones required thousands of skilled stone masons. When the government contracts closed down, craftsmen returned to their homes in all sections of Palestine and introduced the stone column into house architecture, making a building unlike anything found in earlier periods.

Politics was another field of study in which Solomon had a Ph.D. His reign began with a theophany as had the administrations of Moses and Joshua. God said, "Ask what I shall give thee"; to which Solomon responded with a "thank You" for all that You did for my father, David. Then confessing his own inability to rule without God's help he pleads: "Give thy servant therefore an understanding heart to judge thy people, that I may discern between good and evil; for who is able to judge this thy great people?" (I Kings 3:9). This prayer differed strikingly from the common pagan prayers we see in archaeological inscriptions and other records. The latter are excellently condensed in I Kings 3:11-12. "And God said unto him, Because thou hast asked this thing, and hast not asked for thyself long life, neither hast asked riches for thyself, nor hast asked the life of thine enemies, but hast asked for thyself understanding to discern justice; behold, I have done according to thy word."

So-called pools of Solomon. They were built by Pontius Pilate.
© *Matson Photo Service*

Solomon's emphasis on peace is seen in that he permitted the fringes of the new empire which David had created to slip away without a military struggle. Although he was a man of peace, he still believed in military preparedness for Palestine proper and he added the chariot to the nation's military equipment. Excavations at Megiddo have uncovered the remodeling of his chariot depots with stalls for 450 horses plus parade grounds, etc. David, for some reason unknown to us, did not emphasize chariot warfare. Solomon also rebuilt the fortresses of Hazor, Megiddo and Gezer. Since Solomon's reign was essentially an epoch of peace, Israel reached her peak of material culture at that time.

Solomon remodeled the federal government by replacing the original tribal unit with twelve new geographic areas, directly responsible to Solomon only. Some of the new units followed the old boundary lines, others did not. Franklin D. Roosevelt, while president, attempted something like Solomon's federal divisions but was unable to get it ratified by Congress.

Solomon did well in international affairs. He intermarried into Egypt, which is an ancient diplomatic term for an alliance. Hiram of Tyre was his business partner. Even the Queen of Sheba came from the farthest corner of Arabia to Jerusalem. Business is always an important part of international politics; and she had great riches in gold and incense, which were the rarest items in the commerce of that day. At Bethel we found a pottery stamp used by the merchants of the Queen of Sheba to stamp their signatures on the bags of incense. It dates about a century after the visit of the Queen of Sheba to Solomon.

Solomon controlled all the caravan trade on the eastern desert's edge from Palmyra to Aqabah at least during most of his reign. Hiram of Tyre dominated Mediterranean Sea commerce but Solomon had him join Israel in a maritime venture down the Red Sea and around the shoulder of Africa. Egypt, which was a major manufacturing center, had to pay taxes to Solomon on her goods that must needs go north through his kingdom to reach Anatolian and Mesopotamian markets. The Hittites from Asia Minor sold him horses, which he in turn resold at a profit to Egypt.

His proverbs often refer to business matters. Here is a variety of themes in that field. "A false balance is an abomination to Yahweh; But a just weight is his delight" (11:1). "He that is surety for a stranger shall smart for it; But he that hateth suretyship is secure" (11:15). "The liberal soul shall be made fat; And he that watereth shall be watered also himself" (11:25). "Whoso mocketh the poor reproacheth his Maker; And he that is glad at calamity shall not be unpunished" (17:5). "He also that is slack in his work is brother to him that is a destroyer" (18:9). "The rich ruleth over the poor; And the borrower is servant to the lender" (22:7). Some of the most significant of these proverbs on the ancient and modern problems of poverty are as follows, "He that oppresseth the poor reproacheth his Maker; But he that hath mercy on the needy honoreth him" (14:31). "He that hath pity upon the poor lendeth unto Yahweh, And his good deed will he pay him again" (19:17). "The rich and the poor meet together: Yahweh is the maker of them all" (22:2). Unfortunately in his later years, Solomon repudiated many of his own proverbs.

Just as politics and business cannot be separated, so neither can good government and psychology. Solomon was certainly a Ph.D. in this field, a psychologist par excellence. Read I Kings 3:16-28 for his first court decision, remembering that an Israelite judge did not simply pass judgment on the evidence presented by the opposing parties in the case, but the judge himself must ask questions in such a way that one of the litigants would demonstrate his innocence and the other would demonstrate his guilt. This was where Solomon was a genius. Since Solomon was king he was the final court of appeals.

Most of the book of Proverbs shows a good appreciation of psychology at its best. Here is a variety of striking verses. "Walk with wise men, and thou shalt be wise; But the companion of fools shall smart for it" (13:20). "A rebuke entereth deeper into one that hath understanding than a hundred stripes into a fool" (17:10). "Whoso rewardeth evil for good, Evil shall not depart from his house" (17:13). "Even a fool, when he holdeth his peace, is counted wise; When he shutteth his lips, he is esteemed as prudent" (17:28). "Whoso findeth a wife findeth a good thing, And obtaineth favor of Yahweh" (18:22). "Bread of falsehood is sweet to a man; But afterwards his mouth shall be filled with gravel" (20:17). "Buy the truth, and sell it not; Yea, wisdom, and instructions, and understanding" (23:23). "Rejoice not when thine enemy falleth, And let not thy heart be glad when he is overthrown" (24:17).

Solomon was also at home in theology. He made one of the most significant prayers found in all of Scripture, when he dedicated the temple (I Kings 8). Seven times he used such phrases as "when they shall pray toward this place." This was the Old Testament way of praying in the name of Christ. It was looking toward Jerusalem, as under Moses they looked toward the brazen serpent, and as we now look toward the crucified Christ. The ancient Israelites were justified by faith in the promised Messiah (typified in this temple and its ritual). Remember how Daniel prayed thus toward Jerusalem.

In spite of all his Ph.D.'s Solomon flunked one of the super-important courses in the Old Testament University, namely "Israelite homelife." (His father David had also flunked this course.) "And he (Solomon) had seven hundred wives, princesses, and three hundred concubines; and his wives turned away his heart. For it came to pass, when Solomon was old, that his wives turned away his heart after other gods; and his heart was not perfect with Yahweh his God, as was the heart of David his father. For Solomon went after Ashtoreth the goddess of the Sidonians, and after Milcom the abomination of the Ammonites . . . Wherefore Yahweh said unto Solomon, Forasmuch as this is done of thee, and thou hast not kept my covenant and my statutes, which I have commanded thee, I will surely rend the kingdom from thee, and will give it to thy servant" (I Kings 11:3-11).

Unfortunately Solomon is typical of all too many modern Christians in that he failed to practice what he preached. He outlived his faith. Mammon replaced God, and Solomon was no sooner dead than his kingdom was rent asunder. Still more tragic, he lost his first love and asked Yahweh to share a place with the heathen gods of his harem. And these pagan temples were built on the Mt. of Olives directly across the Kidron valley from Solomon's temple to Yahweh.

Nevertheless Christ Himself put such a high value on Solomon's book of Proverbs that it is reflected everywhere in the gospels. If you only knew your Proverbs by

heart and your gospels equally well, you would have a
new appreciation of Solomon. Since Solomon's book was
modern enough for Christ it is modern enough for us.

*   *   *   *

For additional archaeological data see W. F. Albright,
Archaeology and the Religion of Israel, pp. 130-155.

Civil War Then and Now

CHAPTER VII

Civil War Then and Now

A dagger blade

Seventy years of prosperity for any tiny ancient country was too long, so the odds of history favored trouble for Israel as soon as Solomon died. His mania for de luxe government buildings not only in Jerusalem but in the capitals of his new federal districts drained both the farmer and the city man of wealth and workmen. Even the great financial sums amassed by David in his extensive conquests were exhausted, and expenses had to be met by heavy taxes. Solomon had also introduced the corvée, using foreigners in Israel; but this was not enough man-power and so Israelites were drafted for the hated corvée, which had caused their ancestors to flee from Egyptian tyranny.

It was therefore only natural that at Solomon's death there would be an instant repudiation of his economic and manpower policies. The crucial problem was — would this crisis wreck the federal state? His bullheaded son, Reho-boam, refused to adjust to this desperate crisis and so an Israelite labor leader engineered a revolution of the north-ern tribes. Jeroboam is as modern as today and even more so. He had been originally in charge of Solomon's corvée but had been forced to flee to Egypt to save his life. Now he returned and successfully led the revolt against Rebo-boam and Judah. This labor leader made himself king. In modern politics the labor leader is only a "king-maker."

This political problem was in some ways quite simi-lar to the David—Ish-bosheth one, except that Israel and Jeroboam are now the dominant powers. The clergy again took prominent part. The prophet Ahijah gave Jeroboam God's blessing on the revolt, and Shemaiah was able to avert civil war for a time. Both kings, however, became typical Gentile rulers.

Jeroboam, like Judas, had a magnificent opportunity to carry out God's work but, like Saul, he knew a better way to handle government problems than God did. Jero-boam chose a religious syncretism — an impossible blend of Jehovah-Baal worship. Jeroboam correctly feared that if Israel were allowed to go regularly to Yahweh's temple in Jerusalem that faith would triumph over taxes and the nation would quickly be unified; as of course, it should have been. So he erected two rival sanctuaries to Jerusalem, with golden bulls taking the place of the ark of Yahweh as thrones for the invisible Yahweh. He also created a new non-Levitical priesthood and changed the church calendar. The essence of this heresy was that the unity of the Messianic people and their worship was destroyed for two centuries.

God's judgment came quickly on both Jeroboam and Rehoboam. Shishak, Pharaoh of Egypt, came up into Palestine and helped himself to both kingdoms, adding them to his empire. Shishak recorded his victories over 150 of these cities on one of the temple walls at Karnak, where you can still read the story today. Billboards and braggadocio are as old as antiquity. Jeroboam after his Egyptian experience had expected Shishak's blessing, but instead he had to flee to the mountain fastness of Gilead. Shishak also desecrated and plundered Solomon's temple.

The northern kingdom of Israel quickly became a typical Gentile absolute monarchy, including papal power over the new religion and its sanctuaries. Yahweh and the Bible were there in name only to the aristocrats, although "many of the common people" still followed Yahweh faithfully, even to using the Jerusalem sanctuary. Military might, not God, became the final court of appeal in the northern kingdom. If we condense the Bible text into newspaper headlines we have something like the following. Jeroboam dies after 22-year reign. King Nadab assassinated by his General Baasha. King Elah, while dead-drunk, is killed by General Zimri. Zimri reigns 7 days, sets his palace afire and burns to death. Ahab marries Jezebel, uniting Phoenicia and Israel.

In this wedding Jezebel was the power on the throne. She was a true daughter of her high priestly father, who had murdered the king of Tyre and then usurped his throne. Jezebel, of course, insisted on Tyrian Baalism as Israel's religion. Then Elijah and Elisha came on the scene and two of God's major prophets again make a futile attempt to turn the northern kingdom back to Judah.

Under Jeroboam II the kingdom knew one brief period of political power and prosperity, but shortly after his death Tiglath-pileser III of Assyria added three-fourths of the northern kingdom to his empire, and exempted only a small area around the capital city, Samaria. The last six Israelite kings reigned only twenty-five years and then in 721 B.C. Sargon II incorporated the last of Israel into the Assyrian empire, and the northern kingdom disappeared forever.

In our own century we, like ancient Israel, have likewise done rather well ourselves in destroying the power of the Church. Communism is infinitely more successful than Jezebel or Assyria ever were. This century opened with the Russian Orthodox Church having the strongest membership and the greatest political influence in all the orthodox world. Today that church's influence is only a shadow, although there is a true remnant in Russia. For one of the very few times in all of human history a nation has been able to get along politically without any concept of deity. Furthermore she has been anti-everything moral; but in doing so Russian Communism has become one of the two dominant powers in the world! Lenin succeeded where Jeroboam, Jezebel and Tiglath-pileser III failed.

Our century has also seen Luther's homeland "heil a Hitler," who put on a killing program that would have been thrilling joy to Jezebel or any Assyrian monarch. The German Church, like the Russian, was powerless as a political or moral force. It is no wonder that some historians now speak of our times as a post-Christian era in Europe. History has never seen as many people killed in war, or as many refugees fleeing across the face of the earth as in our day.

Remember that World War I, which triggered all this cataclysm, was a war between Christian nations! Furthermore, these Christian nations brought into this holocaust all their subject peoples. Thus they converted Mohammedans, Buddhists, Hindus, animists, etc. into disciples of the god of war. The awful tragedy is that they never seriously tried to convert them to Jesus Christ!

In our own country the Negro is all too often still a social outcast, as was the leper of Christ's time; and yet our civil war was to have settled that a century ago. And most tragic of all, the Bible belt of America is the South. In northern cities, however, we have likewise failed in this as in most other social problems. Nor is Zimri dead in America. I heard a high school boy say to his friend the other day, "Oh, I wish it were Saturday so I could get drunk."

The moral of this period of Israel's history is that the Church's failure in economic stewardship can easily become the Church's suicide. Although, God be thanked, there are always "7,000 who have not bowed the knee to Baal."

*　　*　　*　　*

For additional archaeological data see W. F. Albright, *The Biblical Period from Abraham to Ezra,* Chapters VI and VII.

Elijah, the Abraham Lincoln
of the Israelites

Chapter VIII

Elijah, the Abraham Lincoln of the Israelites

A fertility goddess

When talking to young people I often speak of Moses as the George Washington of the Jews and of Elijah as their Abraham Lincoln. The book of Kings in Hebrew was written on a single scroll, for Hebrew was written with consonants only. But when it was translated into Greek, which specializes in vowels, then two scrolls were

necessary and that is why the English Bible has I and II
Kings. If you were using the original Hebrew scroll of
Kings you would find that approximately the center third
of the book concentrates on two men, Elijah and Elisha!
This shows their importance. But a still better test is to
check every feature of the lives and works of these two
men against the life of Christ and note the parallels!

From Abraham to the Babylonian captivity represents
about thirteen centuries of Israelite history, all of which
can be summarized in a single question put by Elijah to
the Israelites on Mt. Carmel. "How long go ye limping
between the two sides? if Yahweh be God, follow him; but
if Baal, then follow him" (I Kings 18:21). The local settings change, the characters come and go, nations rise and
fall; but the theme of Israel's history remains the same —
Yahweh or Baal, just as since New Testament times it
has been Jesus or Athena.

The Israel of Elijah's day was in many ways quite
similar to that of the United States about the time of our
Civil War, if you will eliminate manufacturing from Israel.
(That did not come in for more than another century.)
The northern kingdom was the breadbasket for Phoenicia
which had only a minimum of farm land but specialized
in manufacturing and shipping. She was the Great Britain
of her day.

Omri was the first strong king in Israel and he was
able to make himself still stronger through alliances with
both Phoenicia and Judah. From now on the Assyrian
records refer to Israel as "the house of Omri," although
that dynasty was quickly gone. Omri moved the capital
to Samaria, and when the work was completed it became
one of the best fortified cities of Palestine. The Assyrians
captured it only after a three-year siege.

Two extensive campaigns of excavations have been carried on here and they have uncovered many details of the city's history. Samaria occupied an isolated hilltop easy of defense. At least some of the Israelite city walls were the casemate type, a military importation from the Hittites. Two fairly thin walls were joined together by cross walls every few meters and this gives the appearance of a long series of small rooms. Each room was probably filled with earth. Much of the wall was a normal twelve foot Palestinian wall but at one place it was thirty-two feet wide. Sections of the Omri-Ahab palace and its later remodeling by Jeroboam II have been found. This palace area was just over three hundred feet long. It followed the common plan of Near Eastern palaces, i.e. series of two-story buildings erected around open courts. At the side of one courtyard is an excellently constructed rectangular pool 33 x 17 feet. One naturally conjectures that this may have

The ruins of Omri's Palace in Samaria. © *Matson Photo Service*

been the pool near where the dogs licked up the blood from the chariot that carried dead Ahab home (I Kings 22: 35-38).

Many ivory inlays were found in the palace complex. They came from the inlaid wall paneling of wood and from inlaid furniture and toilet articles (I Kings 22:39; Amos 6:4). This work was doubtless done by Phoenician craftsmen who patterned their work after Egyptian and Syrian originals. Writing of any type is a rare find in Palestine but Samaria yielded 63 ostraca. These inscribed potsherds from the royal archives served as tax receipts and business documents. They show that the old federal districts created by Solomon were still intact in the northern kingdom.

Sargon II, the conqueror of Samaria, rebuilt it and made it the capital of an Assyrian province. Persia continued it as a district capital and at that time even Jerusalem was under its control. The city was captured by Alexander the Great and converted into a Greek city. Its original Samaritan population was deported to Shechem. The city was again destroyed by the Maccabees but it was strong again under the Romans.

It was embellished by Herod the Great who erected here a magnificent temple to his political patron, Augustus Caesar. He renamed the city Sebaste after Caesar. (Sebaste is the Greek equivalent for the Latin Augustus.) Here the Greek population of Samaria worshiped Augustus Caesar as a god! This is the same Herod the Great who built the great Jerusalem temple in which Christ worshiped. Herod was a master politician and could at any time become all things to all men.

Now to return to Omri. His son married Jezebel, the fanatical Baal worshiper, who insisted that Israel worship

Baal, the Canaanite storm god, holding the forked lightning as a spear. *Kelso*

Wilderness of Judaea in a season of drought. *Kelso*

her gods as well as Yahweh. Into this crisis came Elijah. He chose Mt. Carmel as a perfect setting for his work. Here both the Canaanites and the Phoenicians worshiped Baal, the giver of fertile farmlands, and Ashera, goddess of the sea. What an appropriate setting, for Carmel means literally the garden spot, and this mountain is a great headland jutting out into the sea. The story of Yahweh's victory here is so condensed in Scripture that it must be read *in toto*. See I Kings 18:16-46. Elijah is king for a day! Little Ahab cringed before him and could only do the prophet's bidding.

As Yahweh justified Himself against Baal in Joshua's day, so it was the same at Carmel. It is Yahweh's lightning and not Baal's; it is Yahweh's rain and not Baal's. The wages of sin is death; and the 450 prophets of Baal and the 400 prophets of Ashera are slaughtered at the base of Carmel beside the river Kishon, the same stream which, swollen by Yahweh's cloudbursts, drowned the hosts of Sisera. Finally, look at your map and note Elijah's marathon run before the chariot of Ahab from Carmel to Jezreel. What a blend of the physical and the spiritual in Elijah! Alas, he has too few descendants. The drought referred to in this episode was so critical that it is actually mentioned by writers from the Phoenician capital at Tyre.

When Jezebel heard the news, murder was her only thought; but Elijah outwitted her and fled to Sinai. Here like Moses he had a theophany; here he too met God personally. From Yahweh he received three commands. He was to anoint Hazael king over Syria, Jehu king over Israel and Elisha as his successor. Remember that God always runs national and international secular history as well as church history.

Place of sacrifice in Mt. Carmel called in Arabic, El-Mahraqua, "The Place of Burning." © *Matson Photo Service*

The Naboth episode illustrates that even in the northern kingdom the old Mosaic land laws were still valid in all real estate transactions. According to these laws farm land could not be sold outside the family circle. Naboth the commoner, refused to sell his ancestral property to King Ahab, but the pagan Jezebel solved the dilemma for her husband by having Naboth killed and his land confiscated by the crown. God, however, always makes the last move and He promised Jezebel that the dogs would eat her body near this very field; and they did. Contrast her death with that of Elijah's chariot ride to heaven!

Elijah and Lincoln both appeared at a watershed in their nation's history. Each had to make a choice involving the whole concept of national life — to follow the old path or to cater to selfish partisan policies. With Elijah it involved both church and state; with Lincoln it was state only. Baalism went down with Jezebel, or more accurately it phased off from sensualism into secularism and finally into political death. Both Elijah and Lincoln held to a theory of state where all men are equal and where that state must be kept intact to preserve that equality.

Neither man fitted the ecclesiastical pattern of his day. Elijah completely ignored Jerusalem and its sanctuary. No clergy pattern fitted him. He used only his Bible. There was no other like him until John the Baptist. The world was Elijah's parish but God seemed to be his only intimate friend. Lincoln also was completely outside the church pattern of his day although he was on good terms with God and he certainly knew and practiced the Book. Outside of the United States today Lincoln is not only the most respected American in history but he has no close competitor. Christ's evaluation of Elijah is seen in Elijah's presence at the transfiguration.

In their successors, however, Elijah and Lincoln part company. No one was big enough to step into Lincoln's shoes and the nation suffered greatly from that absence. Elisha, however, wore Elijah's sandals and they were an excellent fit.

Elijah and Elisha are a perfect demonstration that the Church needs different human temperaments for the same time and the same task. Reread the gospels looking for the similarities in the ministry of Christ with the ministries of Elijah and Elisha. Then realize that such ministries must be the ministries of today. The ministry of the pulpit and the pew must always be both timely and timeless.

Jonah Didn't Believe in Foreign Missions Either

CHAPTER IX

Jonah Didn't Believe in Foreign Missions Either

A mace head typical of the time of Jonah

The book of Jonah is often interpreted today as if it were fiction. But the archaeologist finds it much easier to read the book as fact. Jonah's home town was Gath-hepher on the hills near Nazareth in Galilee; so when Jesus refers to Jonah, remember this common geographic missionary homeland.

Detail of the Black Obelisk of Shalmanezer III, recording the tribute of King Jehu. It shows Jehu (top panel) bowing before the Assyrian king. This is the only contemporary picture we have of an Israelite king. *British Museum*

Ahab, Jezebel and Elijah were the dramatic background for Jonah. Ahab was at Ramoth-Gilead where every prophet had promised him victory except Micaiah, who predicted the king's death. Ahab was worried by Micaiah's message and so went into battle in disguise. A chance arrow, however, brought his death as the prophet promised. Jezebel had an equally dramatic end. She was tossed out of the palace window and trampled to death by Jehu's horses. The usurper, Jehu, however, was powerless before the great Shalmaneser III, king of Assyria and he was only too glad to pay the Assyrian tribute and escape with his life. In this invasion, Shalmaneser had come down from Damascus through the Bashan district, plundering, burning and destroying its "countless cities." He then crossed over the Jordan River at Beth-shean and marched to the Mediterranean, via the plains of Jezreel and Esdrae-lon.

On the hills above the latter plain, Jonah looked down on the Assyrian soldiers slaughtering the Israelite population and plundering everything in sight. Since Gath-hepher and the other hill cities were on the flanks of the army, they also probably suffered equally with those of the plains. Then Shalmaneser came to Mt. Carmel and carved his inscription of victory on that mountain — the very same Mt. Carmel where Yahweh had triumphed over Baal and Jezebel only a few years before!

If you take the book as fact, Jonah's actions are perfectly plain. He himself had been an eyewitness to the horror of an Assyrian invasion. Here are some of their inscriptions.

"I crushed the corpses of their warriors in the battle that caused their overthrow. I made their blood to flow over all the ravines and high places of mountains. I cut off their heads and piled them up at the walls of their cities like heaps of grain.

"A pyramid of heads in front of his city I erected. Their young men and women I burned in a bonfire.

"They hung their corpses on gibbets, stripped off their skins, and therewith covered the wall of the city."

Doubtless many of Jonah's relatives were killed or made prisoners. All the foodstuffs which would keep the remaining Israelite families alive for the next year had been drained off by the enemy. And all this had been done in sight of that Mt. Carmel where God had justified Elijah!

When God asked Jonah to preach damnation to Nineveh, a key city of Assyria, he refused to go, for he knew only too well that God usually preaches damnation and salvation in the same sermon.

The traditional tomb of Jonah in Nineveh, the Yunis Mound, in Iraq, Ancient Babylon. © *Matson Photo Service*

So Jonah went down to Jaffa and set sail for Tarshish, probably on the Atlantic coast of Spain near the mouth of the Guadalquivir River. The length of the voyage, plus the technical Hebrew term for a decked-over ship that is used here, means that Jonah was traveling on a well-built large ship. She may have been powered by sail only, although on important business auxiliary oar power was used in calm weather. The ship would carry a large mainmast and small foremast, both using square sails. Great oars mounted over the stern served as rudders.

We can only conjecture the size of Jonah's ship but the best geographers estimate it about 250 tons. The flagship of Columbus was only 100 tons and Magellan's only slightly larger. Vasco de Gama used a ship of 200 tons. A day's sail in antiquity would probably be about 55 nautical miles. These ships were well-built and could stand the bad Mediterranean storms as is shown by the experience of the ship in which Paul sailed. Ezekiel 27:3-9 gives an excellent description of a ship used by the royalty of Tyre. Phoenician cargoes are listed in verses 12-25 of the same chapter.

Almost 250 years after Jonah the Phoenicians probably circumnavigated Africa. This cannot be demonstrated but if they sailed from east to west there are no special oceanography problems against them. An old dry-dock 130 feet long at Athens demonstrates the size of the Greek war vessels, which were smaller than cargo ships. Lucian mentions a large Alexandrian grain ship 180 feet long. It would have a capacity of about 1200 tons. Paul's ship was also an Alexandrian one and carried 276 in its crew and passenger list. Josephus was in a shipwreck when there were 600 persons on board. Underwater archaeology is a fascinating new field of research. French divers have studied the old stone docks at the city of Tyre which are now all under water. A Mycenaean ship loaded with copper has been studied in detail on the ocean floor off the coast of Turkey. One of the ships found off the Mediterranean coast of France of New Testament times was probably 100 feet long.

When Jonah sailed for Tarshish, this was exactly the antithesis of God's geographic orders. Jonah soon found himself caught in a cyclonic storm similar to the one described in Paul's shipwreck. To appreciate Jonah's storm reread Acts 27:14-41. The ship's crew was of many nationalities and each sailor prayed to his own god but there was no answer. In desperation the sailors took the last resort, i.e. they cast lots. Jonah was found to be the guilty party and at his own request, he was tossed into the sea. The sailors were typical pagans for in talking with Jonah they had said, "What shall we do to *you* that the sea may be calm to *us*?" And speaking to God they said, "We beseech thee, let us not perish for this man's life, and lay not upon us innocent blood; for thou, O Yahweh, hast done as it pleased thee" (Jonah 1:14). Notice that their gods had no more ethics than the sailors themselves, i.e. desire equals ethics.

To the man of little faith "the fish story" is too much. But if you have ever known God personally in great and awful crises you will have no trouble with miracles. If you have not had these experiences, then no one can reason you into miracles. The *big* miracle anyway is Jonah's prayer inside the sea monster, not that animal itself. Read that prayer carefully. In conclusion Jonah expresses his thanksgiving to God vowing that he would actually offer sacrifices, i.e. he would yet get ashore somehow and by God's grace go to church! His faith triumphed and God spared his life. He found himself ashore but only to be ordered to Nineveh in the identical words of the first summons.

Nineveh was the second largest of the ancient Mesopotamian cities; only Babylon was larger. Nineveh had not yet reached its peak in Jonah's day; but the city's walls were about eight miles in circumference. Suburbs, however, reached as far as the large city of Calah about fifteen miles away. This expanded Nineveh is the probable city of Jonah's day, where the city is spoken of as a three day's journey. The idiom, "three days," however, may simply mean a big city. Aristotle refers to a statement which mentioned that at the time of Babylon's capture, three days passed before all the city had the news. The reference to 120,000 children, i.e. persons that could not distinguish the left hand from the right, would mean about 600,000 population, a reasonable number for greater Nineveh.

Sennacherib made Nineveh the capital of the Assyrian empire at the end of the 8th century B.C. Note that the king in the book of Jonah is only the king of Nineveh, not the king of Assyria. Ashurbanapal, the last great Assyrian king, collected the finest library in the ancient Near East at Nineveh; and it is a major source of our knowledge of ancient Mesopotamia. It was the forerunner of the still more famous library at Alexandria in Egypt. The archaeologists know the details of about two millennia of Nineveh's history, although it was founded much earlier. Its cult of Ishtar, goddess of love and war, was famous as far away as Egypt long before the time of Moses.

Jonah's message was damnation; forty days and Nineveh will be destroyed. This message he preached with such enthusiastic sincerity that the whole city from slave to king repented. They even dressed their animals in the black sackcloth of mourning. So sincere was the king that he ordered the populace "let them cry mightily unto God; yea, let them turn everyone from his evil way, and from the violence that is in his hands." And God accepted the repentance of the city.

But what about Jonah? The last chapter of the book is probably the poorest translation in the Bible. Let us paraphrase a little of it into modern English. "And Jonah was so angry that he was burnt up and he said to God, 'Isn't this just what I told you in my home-town? That's why I left for Tarshish, because I knew you were a forgiving God and merciful, holding your anger and over-flowing in grace. And I knew that you would spare them. Please God, kill me. I would rather be dead than alive!' And God said, 'Come on now, Jonah, does this red-hot anger do you any good?' "

Jonah refused to answer God. Instead he walked over to the east of the city to watch Nineveh go up in smoke like Sodom and Gomorrah. The only burning, however, was the hot sun on Jonah's head; and beginning to swoon he said, "I would rather be dead than alive. Yes, it does me good to be angry, even if it kills me!"

But God reminded Jonah that God does indeed love the Gentiles just as truly as the Jews; and He will instantly pardon any sinner be he person or nation, be he Jonah or Nineveh. The Ninevites brought forth works meet for repentance; but Jonah, even after God had twice saved him from death, refused to be a partner in foreign missions. Jonah saw only the sinners in Nineveh, forgetting that the vast percentage of Israel's population for the last century had been almost as ungodly as Assyria!

Jonah's descendants are probably the most numerous group that you can find in every Christian Church today!

They may give a pittance to missions, but essentially Christianity is for middle-class Americans only. In Jonah's day, God was for Jews only, as Christ is for us only today. We see the wickedness in Communism today but not the wickedness of our own nation, although God has blessed us more than any nation with the possible exception of ancient Israel. At the turn of the century, the various boards of foreign missions pleaded for missionaries for Japan and China. American Christians would not give their sons to missions and so a new Assyria arose whose name was Japan, and then American Christians had to give their sons by the tens of thousands to their nation. And China — unevangelized China — who knows her future, and ours? Unless we pray in dead earnest, "Thy kingdom come, Thy will be done," tragedy awaits both of us.

But there were more sinners than Jonah. Alas, Assyria's repentance was but for a day. As the drug addict returns to his heroin, so Assyria soon returned to her sins. A new prophet speaks to them. Nahum is now God's agent, not of grace but for doom; and Assyria is wiped off the face of the earth and none to mourn her. "Thy shepherds slumber, O king of Assyria; thy nobles are at rest; thy people are scattered upon the mountains, and there is none to gather them. There is no assuaging of thy hurt; thy wound is grievous: all that hear the report of thee clap their hands over thee; for upon whom hath not thy wickedness passed continually?" (Nahum 3:18-19).

We might rethink Matthew 7:21-23. "Not everyone that saith unto me, Lord, Lord, shall enter into the kingdom of heaven; but he that doeth the will of my Father who is in heaven. Many will say to me in that day, Lord, Lord, did we not prophesy by thy name, and by thy name cast out demons, and by thy name do many mighty works? And then will I profess unto them, I never knew you: depart from me, ye that work iniquity."

After these words the Church should not make sport of Jonah until we can evangelize Russia. And even then God will have to be as gracious to us as He is to Russia! Why should Christ have to wait over 1900 years to see the Church appreciate His Gospel enough to take that Gospel to all mankind? Remember that today there are more lost souls than ever before in the world's history. Any doctor who will discover a cure for cancer and then refuse to share it with his patients and his fellow doctors would be the most hated man in the world. We have Jesus Christ; why do we withhold life from the living dead!

Amos, a Salvation Army Preacher

CHAPTER X

Amos, a Salvation Army Preacher

Bird bone used to apply eye paint

The Salvation Army is over a hundred years old and going strong, for it is the one Christian denomination that all the unfortunate of earth can best understand and love. Such a Salvation Army preacher was Amos some 2700 years ago. He repudiated any prophetic title and thought of himself as an ordinary layman, whose chief business was to work for God. He earned a living by shepherding. Thus he fits the Salvation Army pattern perfectly.

He left us only one sermon but that one was magnificent and immortal. Seldom will you ever hear as perfect a twenty-minute sermon as this one; and remember that he preached it in *poetry,* not prose! Although Amos was dealing with the social problems of the mid-eighth century B.C. in Palestine, his presentation of the problem and its solution is far superior to most modern speakers. He too, like ourselves, was caught in an industrial revolution that all too often ignored God. But in Amos God found a spokesman for that new manufacturing age and for ours also.

Some scholars see his book as snatches of various sermonettes blended together, but it is far more reasonable to take the whole book as one single sermon and its political aftermath. This Salvation Army preacher is inseparable from his message. He was a shepherd and that vocabulary appears everywhere in his preaching. The great out-of-doors was both his home and his vocabulary. He raised a special breed of sheep famous for its wool; and this product he sold to the highest bidder. Bethel was a luxury city which appreciated fine wool, and on this occasion it served both as a market for his wool and as a pulpit for his sermon. That city was located on the great north and south ridge road of western Palestine, which was one of the trade routes that handled commerce between Africa and Asia Minor. Here he picked up world news from international traveling men, who are always one of the best judges of political movements. Amos was still better in conversations with God; and God is always the best center of all information.

I spent four summers in the excavations of Bethel and

The mountain top in the center is part of the original mountain top high place where the Canaanite god El was worshiped about 3500 B.C. This site later became the city of Bethel and was so named in honor of El. The walls belong to the city gate about the time of Joseph. *Kelso*

worked in the period of Amos each season. Jeroboam's temple was of course the first thing we looked for; and we were still searching for it when we quit work. But it eluded us. It is most likely under the houses of the modern town of Beitin just north of the two big springs which are the reason for the existence of Bethel. Ancient temples are often built beside springs. Unfortunately city property is too expensive for excavations.

We did, however, find a mountain top open-air high place where the Canaanite god El was worshiped at least as early as 3500 B.C. It was this god who gave his name to the city. The white limestone ledge was in many places stained with the blood of the animals sacrificed here, preserved by the wet clay in the debris above it. The F.B.I. test for blood was positive on all these dark stains but the plain white limestone gave no reaction. In the debris above the high place were fragments of many animal bones and hundreds of flints used in butchering these animals. Surgeons at Jerusalem examined these bones but found no sign of human sacrifice here. The debris also contained a great amount of broken pottery from the vessels used to cook the sacrifices and at one place the limestone ledge had been calcined where they had built their sacrificial fires. It is the Canaanite theology from this old high place that Jeroboam I blended into the Yahweh worship at his Bethel sanctuary.

The great city wall which surrounded the city and was used throughout its history was built shortly after the time of Joseph. It averaged about twelve feet in width and was constructed of massive stones interlocked together. This section of the wall was originally about twenty feet high and above that rose another ten feet of mud-dried brick. The base of the wall was protected from battering rams by a wide sloping revetment.

The only city gate preserved from Amos' time was the north gate. Inside of it was an open area which could be used as a meeting place for the law court. Amos more likely spoke at the west or the south gate. The former is destroyed down into Canaanite times but in the debris outside the gate was found an inscription from the merchants from the Queen of Sheba described in Chapter VI. We could not find the south gate dating to the time of Amos although we did locate the south gate which Christ would have used as He traveled north from Jerusalem to Galilee.

The city was desperately poor in the days of the Judges but quickly turned prosperous under David and Solomon and remained so until its destruction by the Assyrians at the time of Samaria's downfall. Some houses, however, lived through that destruction. The most interesting of these had been used and re-used about three centuries. When its walls were cleared down to the original floor level they stood about eighteen feet high. Here and there one found a slum dwelling and at other times there even appeared something like the header and stretcher walls of the Phoenicians. Most of the homes were built of ordinary field stone. Occasionally a house wall had been toppled by an earthquake and left just as it fell; a new wall was built beside it.

The normal house plan did not change much after the time of David except for the tall stone columns used after the days of Solomon. The average room was small and rectangular in shape. The floors were often beaten earth mixed with powdered lime. The same type of floor is common today in poor homes and country school houses. The best houses had flagstone floors.

We found only a few signs of manufacturing, so commerce and cult must have been the secret of the city's wealth. Bethel was the royal shrine, and that insured good prosperity. This is the city that Elijah and Elisha and Amos all knew personally. Bethel's history reached from 3500 B.C. to A.D. 800. It is mentioned more often in the Old Testament than any other city except Jerusalem.

In ancient Israel the law court was often held at the city gate or the market place; and standing at the city gate of Bethel Amos used the legal pattern of the courtroom as the outline for his sermon. He stressed the following themes.

I. God pronounces a universal sentence of punishment upon all sinful nations (I-II).

II. God declares a specific indictment of Israel's sins (III-IV).

III. God offers Israel a final opportunity to plead guilty of her sins and repent (V:1-15).

IV. God finally pronounces judgment upon a guilty and unrepenting Israel (V:16 - IX).

Amos was a born psychologist. His first problem was to get Israel to condemn herself for "A man convinced against his will is of the same opinion still." So Amos began his message with the theme that God is now ready to judge the *Gentile* nations. He condemned those nations *surrounding Israel*; Damascus for atrocities in war; Gaza for slave trading; Tyre for the same plus violation of treaty; Edom for bloody violation of racial ties; Ammon for crimes against womanhood in war and Moab for desecration of the dead. Note the good TV pattern he used — a flash against Damascus to the NE, then one on Gaza to

the SW, Tyre due N, Edom to the SE, Ammon to the
E and Moab to the SE. Each flash portrayed an atrocity
where *Israel had been the victim*. Meanwhile the audience
would all be thinking "Amen" if not vocalizing it.

Seven is the key item for super emphasis in Hebrew
so his audience would watch for his climax in the seventh
news flash. It was Judah — her sister nation, a people
so wicked in the eyes of the northerners that they had been
forced to revolt from Jerusalem and establish their own
state. In the eyes of Amos, however, Judah's crime was
still more heinous for she had violated not only the laws
of conscience as had the six Gentile nations, but far more
serious, she had blasphemed God. To the audience this
was a perfect climax for the first part of a sermon and
they relaxed to get ready for point two.

But Amos startled them with a super climax, an eighth
criminal. And that was Israel itself! "Thou art the man,"
Amos said to Israel as Nathan had said to David.

Then quickly, before the audience could recover itself,
he reviewed how God had wiped out the original Amorite
population of Palestine for sins involving the violation of
conscience. How much greater would be the doom of
Israel which had violated not only the laws of conscience
but also Yahweh's revelation.

After such a surprising and annihilating attack on
church members as Amos had made, his next remarks
must of necessity be a compelling indictment of Israel's
sin. And it must be fast and crushing so that the congre-
gation could not catch its balance and "change the subject."

"You only have I known of all the families of the
earth; therefore I will visit upon you all your iniquities"
(Amos 3:2). The greater the blessing the greater the
guilt! Verses 3-8 that follow are the shepherd's own vivid

Byzantine ruins of Tekoa, the birthplace of the prophet Amos.
© *Matson Photo Service*

experiences. Even the trumpet blast in the city was the
air-raid siren for the people working in the fields and the
desert.

Tekoa, the home town of Amos, literally meant "the
alarm trumpet." His literary climax is the "lion's roar."
To the shepherd who had intimate experience with the
lions, this meant that the king of beasts had *already* caught
his prey and killed it. He was now ready to devour it.
Tragic words indeed, that Israel heard that day in this
figure of speech. With God, Israel was already as good as
dead nationally. It only remained for Assyria, the lion-
hearted, to devour her at his political leisure.

The crimes that had brought Israel her death sentence were:

Violence and robbery in the palaces — sins against conscience.

False worship in the sanctuaries — sins against Revelation.

A degenerate womanhood — sins against conscience.

A corrupt church — sins against Revelation.

Note the Hebrew climax in a dual repetition: conscience and Revelation, conscience and Revelation. These were the final steps that had taken Israel down the road to perdition. Violence and robbery in the palaces would correspond to a modern supreme court composed of gangsters. Womanhood was so degenerate that it was actually leading the men into deeper sin. So heinous were these crimes that the lion's banquet was again alluded to. From Israel's national carcass there will be left only the equivalent of two shin bones and the rag of an ear. *And Israel had been God's lamb!*

All the time, year after year, God had warned Israel of her sin. Providence had tried again and again to open her eyes to repentance. Read Amos 4:6-11. Now grace is finished. Death is her sentence! "Therefore thus will I do unto thee, O Israel; and because I will do this unto thee, prepare to meet thy God, O Israel" (Amos 4:12). Often the words, "prepare to meet thy God," are used as the text for an evangelistic message. This verse of Scripture, however, says exactly the opposite; this text is damnation not salvation.

Quickly before the audience can reply to this second theme of his sermon, Amos plunges into the third point. First he *sings* one verse of a funeral song. Next he gives the casualty list from the war. Nine out of every ten of

Israel are dead! Then Amos like a true Salvation Army preacher makes one last call for repentance. This is not for the doomed nation as a unit but for any individuals out of that nation who will return to their Lord and Saviour. Like Lot and his family some individuals may escape their nation's Sodom and Gomorrah. Then like any good pastor Amos tells them *how* to repent:

"Seek ye Yahweh and ye shall live.

Seek ye good and not evil that ye may live (i.e. seek to promote good)."

But almost in the same breath Amos concludes his sermon by pronouncing God's judgment upon a guilty and un-repenting Israel:

The day of Yahweh, which Israel would expect to bring blessing to her, shall bring inescapable doom.

False worship cannot avert doom.

The Israel of Palestine shall suffer the same judgment as the Israel of the wilderness, for each worshiped Yahweh *and other gods.*

Finally visions and interludes intensified this message of doom. The introduction of these visions gave Amos an opportunity to vivify and duplicate his message. Israel shall face a famine for the Word of God. The Lord stands in judgment at His altar. No sinful nation, not even His own Israel, can escape the holy and omnipotent Yahweh.

This 2700-year-old sermon is so modern that it needs no further comment. "Let him that hath ears to hear, hear," which in American phraseology means "he that hears, let him *obey!*" Obedience is the mark of God's child in all generations.

Isaiah and Calvin

CHAPTER XI

Isaiah and Calvin

A section of the rich, decorative ivory trim used on furniture and other objects in the time of Isaiah

Perhaps Calvin may not seem like a very modern figure to you, since he has been dead 400 years, but unfortunately the Church has not produced a better Bible scholar and theologian since his day. The reason we have not had better theologians since is because we have not had theologians who are his equal in Bible research.

Isaiah is a long book and as it is primarily the early chapters that best parallel our times we shall concentrate on them. Isaiah was always at home among the political, economic and religious aristocrats of his day — a period reaching from the reign of Uzziah through Hezekiah. This gave him a pastorate of forty or fifty years depending on your date for Sennacherib's invasion. To read Isaiah in the English is to recognize a literary genius and to read him in Hebrew is to enhance that evaluation. Like Solomon he was a man interested in everything and he never lacked for a striking illustration or allusion.

As a boy Isaiah grew up under Uzziah, who from a purely administrative angle was the best all around ruler Judah ever had. When you read Isaiah's vision (Chapter 6) remember that this Uzziah had just died and his coregents Jotham and Ahaz had already demonstrated themselves as powerless persons. Most of the world's throne power was held by Tiglath-pileser III and this Assyrian was soon to add over three-fourths of the northern kingdom to his empire and was breathing down Judah's neck. But in that vision, when the throne of Judah was going down and that of Assyria was going up, God's throne was standing eternal in the heavens. Even now whether or not we pray, "Thy kingdom come, Thy will be done," God's kingdom comes just the same and all nations must always adjust themselves to that King of kings.

It is the sovereignty of God that Isaiah emphasizes and which Calvin echoes. Once you accept the *sovereignty* of God and the *grace* of God (which Isaiah also received here, and which likewise Calvin echoes) then all things are possible. And for the Christian there is no finer demonstration of this dual truth than Paul's life. With greater light than Isaiah had he could add, "It is no longer I that live, but Christ liveth in me."

Excavating the ruins of a house at Kiriath-sepher dating back to the days of Isaiah and Jeremiah. The city was given over primarily to the weaving and dyeing of cloth. The city's casemate walls are seen at right. *Kelso*

Now let us get on to lesser things — earthly things where you and I are more at home. Isaiah saw the beginning of the manufacturing age in Palestine as Jeremiah saw the climax and then the cataclysmic end of all those industries. Here were modern assembly line techniques and here were one-industry towns. The farmers flocked to the industrial cities and the sweat shops absorbed them. Over-supply of labor glutted the market and wages fell to starvation levels.

Micah, a farmer contemporary of Isaiah, attacked the courts for their conniving in the nation's economic crimes. In 3:1-3, using the background of the butchering of sheep and cutting them up for stew, Micah calls these business tycoons and their lawyers cannibals living off of the flesh of their helpless employees. Isaiah echoes this when he says, "Thy princes are rebellious, and companions of thieves; everyone loveth bribes, and followeth after rewards: they judge not the fatherless, neither doth the cause of the widow come unto them" (1:23).

The abandonment of these farms created two other sins. Those who sold their farms thereby violated the Mosaic land laws, which formed a solid basis for the economic structure of society. As long as the farmer owned his own land, he could at least eke out an existence and be a free man rather than a serf or slave. The second sinners were those aristocrats who purchased these lands and ran the farms with serf labor — men rejected by the mill owners. Micah condemns these land sinners, "Woe to them that devise iniquity and work evil upon their beds! when the morning is light, they practise it, because it is in the power of their hand. And they covet fields, and seize them; and houses, and take them away: and they oppress a man and his house, even a man and his heritage"

(Micah 2:1-2). Isaiah echoes it. "Woe to them that join house to house, that lay field to field, till there be no room, and ye be made to dwell alone in the midst of the land!" (Isaiah 5:8).

Isaiah, however, concentrates his wrath primarily on government officials who permit all these economic sins. "Yahweh standeth up to contend, and standeth to judge the peoples. Yahweh will enter into judgment with the elders of his people, and the princes thereof: It is ye that have eaten up the vineyard; the spoil of the poor is in your houses: what mean ye that ye crush my people, and grind the face of the poor? saith the Lord Yahweh of hosts" (Isaiah 3:13-15). The wives of the rich gloat in their luxury but slavery shall be their punishment. "In that day the

The complete scroll of Isaiah, from the Dead Sea Scrolls, opened to chapter 40. The entire scroll consists of 17 sheets of parchment sewn together (see seam at right), and measures 24 feet in length. *Photo courtesy American Schools of Oriental Research, Jerusalem and Baghdad.*

Lord will take away the finery of the anklets, the head-
bands, and the crescents; the pendants, the bracelets, and
the scarfs; the headdresses, the armlets, the sashes, the
perfume boxes, and the amulets; the signet rings and nose
rings; the festal robes, the mantles, the cloaks, and the
handbags; the garments of gauze, the linen garments, the
turbans, and the veils" (Isaiah 3:18-23 RSV). The men
spent their unjust gain on liquor and night life. "Woe
unto them that rise up early in the morning, that they
may follow strong drink; that tarry late into the night,
till wine inflame them! and the harp and the lute, the
tabret and the pipe, and wine, are in their feasts; but they
regard not the work of Yahweh, neither have they considered the operation of his hands" (Isaiah 5:11-12).

Here are the key industries that Isaiah refers to. Ar-
morment (wood, stone, metal, leather), baking, building
trades (stone, brick, lumber, clay and lime), butchering,
ceramics (pottery, crucibles, bricks, furnaces), clothing
(wool, cotton, linen, sackcloth, leather), idols and amulets (wood, stone, metal, clay), jewelry (gold, silver, copper, precious stones), leather (sandals, harness, etc., handbags, shields, water-skins), lumbering (farm tools, door
and window frames, furniture, wagons, chariots), mer-
chandising, metallurgy (copper, bronze, gold, silver, iron,
steel, tin, lead), milling, musical instruments, perfumery,
publishing (papyrus, leather), rope, scribe, i.e. public
stenographer, shipping (land and water), spices, tent and
sail, tomb-maker, wine and hard liquor.

Let us look at one of these industries, namely ceramics.
The best pottery ever produced in Palestine was about the
time of Joseph. Then the potter was an artist. The clay
was skillfully prepared, the throwing on the wheel was
better than the best Greek work and the kiln heat was

just right. Only Chinese ware was better. By Isaiah's time ceramics had become a typical manufacturing business. Because of its constant use and fragile nature, pottery had a very short life. Furthermore pottery was then used for a great variety of purposes where we now use paper and cloth bags, wooden and cardboard boxes and tin cans. So the potter never lacked for customers. His major problem was sale price.

Now big business entered the picture. It cut costs, greatly increased volume and reduced prices. Cooking pots which were a major sales item, demanded such skill in making that most potters imprinted their *trademark* on the handles. Cheaper clays near at hand were now used by modifying their composition and firing the ware at a lower temperature. This also saved fuel. In the manufacture of large bowls, an expensive item, the following technique was used: less skillful throwers were employed and they threw a thick bowl with a heavy wide foot. Then, when this bowl was leather-hard, it was turned down to the desired shape and thinness, much as we turn wood and metal on a lathe. The bowl was then fired very carefully so as not to warp or crack.

Now the assembly line also came in, with each man doing only one particular job for which he was specially trained. The most skillful worker fired the kiln. He must adjust temperature and time to each ceramic form. Three price ranges gave respectively excellent, good and cheap ware. The medium price range sold by far the greatest amount of pottery. This product was comparable, if not superior, to most of our commercial ware of today.

Isaiah summarizes the sins of Judah in the phrases, "Ye rulers of Sodom, ye people of Gomorrah." He also uses the expression, "The ox knoweth his owner, and the ass his master's crib; but Israel doth not know, my people doth not consider" (1:3). In his war on poverty Isaiah did not use the approach of a sociologist or a politician. His only solution was the Messiah. Poverty to him was not a disease; it was only a symptom. Sin was the root-stock, and poverty was only one of its many branches. To Isaiah the antidote to sin was the Messiah, whom we know better as Jesus, the Christ.

The first major flash on this theme is Isaiah 7:10-17. Ahaz was terrified by the mighty Tiglath-pileser III so he planned to surrender to him and thus escape a major national destruction. God tried to dissuade him and offered to work a miracle for Ahaz and thus save Judah. Ahaz sneeringly replied that to think of such a thing was to tempt God. Then God replied (if we may use an expanded modern parlance), "Well, I am going to give you a sign anyway whether you want it or not. Ahaz, you are my anointed, my representative on earth, you may sell out to Assyria, but remember when the ultimate Messiah comes he will be virgin born. You and every other male member of David's posterity may deny me and blaspheme me and betray me, but that matters nothing. The Messiah will be *virgin born*." Neither Jewish nor Gentile king could outwit God then. Neither can any philosopher or theologian do it today.

Isaiah 9:6-7 describes that Messiah perfectly. He is a "Wonderful Counselor." Anyone will admit that Christ was a unique *teacher*. The world is still waiting for His superior, but it will wait in vain! The title "Mighty God" is the best description of His *works*. "Everlasting Father" is the puzzler. Only a doctrine of the Trinity can handle this passage and even then it is an enigma to all scholars since the "Son" is titled "Father." The last description is

"Prince of Peace." The Hebrew word may be translated "peace" in the sense of cessation from war. Its root meaning, however, is "reconciliation," i.e. restoration to the original status. Through this Messiah we have now been restored to the original position of being sons of God — Christ the only begotten of the Father, we the adopted children. Note that Christ's last will and testament is "Peace I leave with you; my peace I give unto you" (John 14:27). Paul cashed in on that will when he said, "It is no longer I that live, but Christ liveth in me" (Galatians 2:20). Matthew 4:15-16 quotes the Messianic theme of Isaiah 9:1-2, when Christ established His ministry at Capernaum. The ultimate and the unique in Messianic prophecy is, of course, Isaiah 52:13-53:12.

Calvin was more at home in business than was Isaiah. On the theme of poverty Calvin differed from Isaiah because he treated both the immediate symptom i.e. poverty, and the root disease of sin. But Calvin did consider sin as the dominant and ultimate problem and to that problem he devoted his life in Bible study, Bible teaching, preaching and practicing. Calvin was also a major civil power in the bustling city of Geneva. He had been trained as a lawyer in France and this training shows up prominently in every phase of his civil and religious life. He had a hand in the writing and enforcement of most civil laws. But Calvin also insisted that preaching was a major form of social reform. Like our modern church leaders he got into quarrels on medicare, labor and management, education, interest rates, etc. He used the WPA policy in his anti-poverty campaign. His economic as well as his religious influence was a major factor in making Geneva prosperous.

As theologians both Isaiah and Calvin had much the

same creed, although each proclaims it in terms of his own personality. Isaiah stresses the broad outlines but Calvin is also interested in the smallest minutia. Both exalt the same God and the same Gospel.

As far as war is concerned Isaiah is far more modern than Calvin. Isaiah leads us through chapter after chapter of war. Many a modern Christian who studies Isaiah carefully for the first time is aghast at the great amount of space devoted to war. But remember that Assyria was the threat to that world that communism is to the world today. Isaiah has major oracles against Assyria, Babylon, Moab, Damascus, Ethiopia, Egypt, Arabia, Tyre, Ephraim, Jerusalem and Edom. At least fifteen other countries large or small also get minor mention.

There are detailed historical chapters on the Assyrian invasion. The attack of Rezin of Syria and Pekah of Israel against Ahaz prompts him to call Tiglath-pileser III to his help; and Ahaz thus becomes a vassal of Assyria. Sargon II is mentioned in Chapter 20 and the long story of Hezekiah and Sennacherib is in Chapters 36-38. Fortunately we also have Sennacherib's version of the campaign.

And as Hezekiah, the Judaean, who had not submitted to my yoke, 46 of his strongholds, fortified cities, and smaller cities of their environs without number, with the onset of battering rams and the attack of engines, mines, breaches, and axes (?) I besieged, I captured. 200,150 people, small and great, male and female, horses, mules, asses, camels, oxen, and sheep without number I brought out of their midst and counted as booty. He himself I shut up like a caged bird in Jerusalem, his capital city; I erected beleaguering works against him, and turned back by command every one who came out of his city gate. The cities which I had captured, from his country I cut off and gave them to Mitinti, King of Ashdod, Padi, King of Ekron, and Sillibaal, King of Gaza, and diminished his land. In addition to the former tribute, their yearly tax, I added a tax as the impost of my overlordship and laid it upon them. As to Hezekiah himself, the fear of the luster of my lordship overcame him and the Urbi and his favorite soldiers, whom he had brought in to strengthen Jerusalem, his capital city, deserted. With 30 talents of gold, 800 talents of silver, precious stones, rouge, *dakkasi,* lapis lazuli, great *angugmi*-stones, beds of ivory, stationary ivory thrones, elephants' hide, ivory, *ushu*-wood, *ukarinnu*-wood, all sorts of objects, a heavy treasure; also his daughters, the women of his palace, male and female musicians he sent after me to Nineveh, my capital city, and sent his messenger to present the gift and to do homage.

Note that Sennacherib does not claim the capture of Jerusalem, simply that Hezekiah paid him tribute.

Isaiah attributes Sennacherib's abandonment of the campaign to the fact that "the angel of Yahweh went forth and smote in the camp of the Assyrians a hundred and four score and five thousand; and when men arose early in the morning, behold these were all dead bodies" (Isaiah 37:36). The word angel in the Old Testament referred not only to what we call superhuman beings but also to natural phenomena. Some scholars think that the destruction may have been caused by the bubonic plague. Herodotus gives us an Egyptian version of a confrontation of the Egyptian and Assyrian armies on Egypt's borders. He says that field mice ate the bow strings and the shield straps of the Assyrians and that thus the Egyptians easily won.

The mouse is the carrier of the bubonic plague and the ancients knew it well. Note that when the Philistines returned the ark, they sent with it votive offering of golden mice and tumors. (The latter are the characteristic signs of that plague.) The Philistines thought that such sympathetic magic would appease Israel's god for the desecration of his ark. Chapter 39 is part of this same Assyrian picture although the casual reader might not recognize it. Merodach-baladan was the ruler of the province of Babylonia. He was always trying to lead a revolt against Assyria and in this instance was seeking an alliance with Hezekiah.

Isaiah speaks of war as God's response to the sins of both Jew and Gentile. But to the Gentile it is punishment, to the Jew chastisement. But Isaiah, like his contemporary Micah, dreamed of a warless world. "And it shall come to pass in the latter days, that the mountain of Yahweh's house shall be established on the top of the mountains, and shall be exalted above the hills; and all nations shall flow unto it. And many peoples shall go and say, Come ye, and let us go up to the mountain of Yahweh, to the house of the God of Jacob; and he will teach us of his ways, and we will walk in his paths; for out of Zion shall go forth the law, and the word of Yahweh from Jerusalem. And he will judge between the nations, and will decide concerning many peoples; and they shall beat their swords into ploughshares, and their spears into pruninghooks; nation shall not lift up sword against nation, neither shall they learn war any more" (Isaiah 2:2-4).

But that warless world has not yet arrived, although in Bible times the Persians and the Romans each gave something of a foretaste of it. Its final consummation is still waiting on foreign missions, when the kingdoms of this world shall become the kingdom of our Lord and

Saviour, Jesus Christ. Isaiah's oracle on Ethiopia (Chapter 18) illustrates the lethargy of the missionary movement. Before 700 B.C. Israel could have evangelized the Sobat River area of the Sudan which is here referred to. In Paul's day Nero dispatched a military expedition to find the source of the Nile River. It reached the Sobat River before being forced to turn back. It was the beginning of the present century before the missionary finally reached the same people!

The finest tribute to Isaiah is John 12:41 which speaks of Isaiah as seeing Christ's glory and speaking of Him.

Apostasies and Reformations

CHAPTER XII

Apostasies and Reformations

One of two limestone lions upon
which an Astarte statue would stand.

History does repeat itself. The cycle of apostasy and
repentance, which was the pattern of Israel in the days
of the Judges was also the pattern of the southern kingdom
of Judah; although ultimately it became apostasy and
suicide, for Jerusalem died by her own hand in 587 B.C.
In the southern kingdom as in the northern, although less

157

Excavation work in progress on the mound at Lachish.
© *Matson Photo Service*

often, the old Canaanite Baalism was blended into the worship of Yahweh. The most blasphemous reigns there were those of Athaliah, Ahaz and Manasseh.

The first abandonment of true worship in the Jerusalem temple was the work of Athaliah. When Ahaziah, king of Judah, was killed by Jehu, Athaliah usurped the throne of Judah and proved to be a true daughter of Jezebel. She failed, however, in her attempt to butcher all the royal sons, for the wife of the high priest rescued Joash. But she made herself queen of Judah for six years and was the nation's only queen. She introduced the Tyrian Baal as the master god of Jerusalem although she seems to have had little influence outside the city. Her death was brought about by the joint action of the priesthood and the army. The first task of Joash her successor was to restore and repair the temple.

The second abandonment of true worship was the action of Ahaz. Terrified by the power of Tiglath-pileser III he voluntarily surrendered, which meant that Assyrian gods must now receive pre-eminent worship in Yahweh's temple. See Chapter XI. Hezekiah's reformation followed the death of Ahaz.

The third blasphemous king was Manasseh. Here everything went bad. Athaliah's action was purely personal, Ahaz's was political, but with Manasseh it was pure devilment. Everything in the way of sin and false worship was practiced even to child sacrifice and the naming of his successor after the Egyptian god Amon. Although he repented in his old age and tried desperately to undo his sin, he failed. Fifty-five years of sin cannot be cancelled out in a death-bed repentance. This is the most tragic of all the facts of sin. A man's repentance has little influence on those he has led into sin! Even the godly Josiah with his reformation could not stem the flood of sin.

The outstanding modern parallels of these blasphemous rulers are, of course, Hitler's Germany and Stalin's Russia. We Americans have always repudiated such actions as Hitler's policies and Russia's atheism. We prefer to pass up such open blasphemies and follow the more subtle substitution of philosophy for theology, preferring the equating of human reason with Revelation. We like the liberalism of the wolf in sheep's clothing. When God says, "My thoughts are not your thoughts neither are my ways your ways," and "No man can come to me except the Father that sent me draw him," we by-pass these truths of God and prefer Athena with her human reasoning.

A man's attitude toward Jesus Christ and the Bible are the quickest tests for the sincere Christian. The two are inseparable. If you throw away the Bible you know nothing of Jesus Christ except for a couple of brief colorless allusions in secular history. Remember — "No Bible, No Christ." The Bible has problems, thousands of them;

and as a seminary professor I spent a lifetime on them. Most of these problems are occasioned by the following: 1. Scarcity of data which leads to multiple possible interpretations. 2. Duplicates or apparent duplicates. The former are often purposeful but the latter are by far the more common. Here you have not duplicates but similarities. This is where much of J E D & P is often sheer guesswork. 3. The failure to recognize that older books like Genesis have in large part been put into a later Hebrew than that in which they were originally written or that of the original oral tradition. This was one of Wellhausen's major blunders. 4. Texts that do not make sense today may make sense tomorrow when we get new light on them. The Ugaritic texts, for example, have given us new grammar, vocabulary and syntax, which have enabled us to translate passages easily, which were once an enigma. 5. Texts are often puzzling simply because the reader does not know the customs and manners behind them. Much of Job is a case in point. 6. Scribal errors in the text do exist; but usually context, versions or some other clue solves the problem. Remember that *no doctrine hangs on a disputed text.*

The crucial point everywhere is the doctrine of inspiration. The Holy Spirit working through men wrote the Bible. But what are the relative parts played by the Holy Spirit and by men? I am reminded here of an experience in my own life. While still in grammar school I became an apprentice to a pharmacist. When I decided to enter college to study for the ministry he wanted me to stay on with him. He even offered to make me a business partner; but when I said that I had no money, he replied that is no problem at all, for I will lend you the money. But even if my name would have appeared on that drug store sign, I would have known that it got there through him alone and not through me.

So with the writing of Scripture. The men were moved by the Holy Spirit and they were partners with the Holy Spirit; but let us be honest and not make the work of men equal to the work of God.

From Abraham to Christ was approximately 1900 years and out of that time and out of that land the Holy Spirit gave us the Old Testament. It is now almost 1900 years since the New Testament was completed — somewhere around A.D. 70 - 85. Now why has not human reason produced another Bible and a better Bible, if there is such a thing as evolution in the Bible and if human authorship is the major factor in inspiration!

Modern heresies, like the heresies of all times, are some form of Baalism — a philosophy of the natural world. That philosophy may be gross and filthy like that of the Canaanites; it may be sophisticated like that of the best of the Greeks; it may be an intellectual impossibility like modern Christian Science; or it may be an ecclesiastical modernism which suavely denies Christ His deity and makes *His* Bible but another book.

Apostasies were followed by reformation. The most famous in Judah were those of Asa, Jehoshaphat, Hezekiah and Josiah. They were each an effective call back to God. These reformations are, of course, a far more practical theme for us to concentrate on, since reformation is our problem today. We have inherited an apostasy. How by God's grace can we change apostasy into evangelism? That is our task.

Asa's reformation began at home, in the royal family where he deposed his mother because of her idolatry to Canaanite deities. He cut down her idol and burned it at the brook Kidron, following something of Moses' pattern at Sinai. Rehoboam's mother had also been a pagan. Asa had to do away with the Sodomite priests and renew the altar before the temple of Yahweh. Constructively he renewed the nation's covenant with God at Jerusalem. Jehoshaphat continued his father's reformation with additional stress on getting priests and civil judges out into the countryside to instruct the common people in the Mosaic law, and to insist on its enforcement.

Hezekiah's reformation was still more strict in removing Baal elements from Israel's life. He also called the nation back from the blasphemous national Assyrian worship which Ahaz had introduced. He both purified and sanctified Yahweh's temple. A special Passover service was held, as if the present crisis paralleled Israel's escape from Egypt. Hezekiah among the aristocracy and Micah among the farmers were the new prophetic helpers. The priesthood and the government needed this new assist and it was a powerful help.

Josiah made the most drastic reformation of all, but the kingdom of Judah was already dying fast. Jeremiah preached to a people of deaf ears, although some of those who heard Christ thought He might be Jeremiah.

These written prophets were the ancestors of what we call evangelists. Modern parallels are Moody, Chapman and Graham, although they play a far less important part in politics than did the Bible preachers. At all costs God must be preached, the Bible must be taught and souls must be saved. This constitutes a Biblical reformation.

Apostasy and reformation, apostasy and reformation, that was the outline of church history in the Old Testament, but finally the circle was always broken. The ultimate end was suicide. In the southern kingdom it was

Top: Crusader castle at Kerak. *Kelso*

Bottom: Modern Kerak from the air. This was the ancient Kir of Moab. *Kelso*

the destruction of Jerusalem. Manasseh sowed sin so widely and for such a long time that at last the southern kingdom, like the northern one, committed the unpardonable sin. God destroyed His own holy city and His own holy temple and exiled His own holy people to Babylonia, from which He had so long ago called Abraham to world evangelism.

Christ still knocks and knocks on the door and waits for entrance. If men will not have His salvation, then their only alternative is damnation. Samaria found it out in 721 B.C.; so did Jerusalem twice (587 B.C. and A.D. 70) and so did Russia only yesterday. What is the handwriting on the wall for an unrepenting U.S.A.? The books of Kings and Chronicles are good reading for any thoughtful Christian!

*   *   *   *

For detailed archaeological data, see W. F. Albright, *The Biblical Period from Abraham to Ezra,* Chapters VII-VIII, and *From the Stone Age to Christianity,* Chapter V.

Cyrus Anticipated the U.S.A.

CHAPTER XIII

Cyrus Anticipated the U.S.A.

The cylinder of Cyrus, telling of his capture of Babylon and his liberations of captive peoples. *British Museum*

In Isaiah God speaks of Cyrus as His shepherd and His anointed i.e., Messiah. These two terms designate Cyrus as a king chosen by God to be His agent in world history. And Cyrus was, indeed, one of history's most significant monarchs. Look at this abridged summary of the Persian empire which Cyrus created. For the first time in history the Persians give us a world empire dominated by Aryans. The previous Hamitic and Semitic world empires had made a tragedy of international government. But Persia brought in a veritable millennium for subject peoples. These Persians were virtually an unknown people until Cyrus in one generation made them masters of the world. Cyrus was at least as great a military genius as Alexander.

To create his empire Cyrus had to capture about twenty strong countries including Lydia where Croesus, the richest man in the world, ruled Asia Minor; and Babylonia, the greatest of the ancient powers before Cyrus. He ruled from the Aegean Sea on the west to the Jaxartes River and the Himalayas on the east. All of these he consolidated into an empire that lasted two centuries. This is the final test of military power and it is here where Alexander was a total failure as his empire fell to pieces immediately upon his death.

Under Darius the Persian empire increased somewhat and was then twice the size of any previous world empire. Darius governed from the Balkans and Egypt on the west well into India on the east. The Persian empire ran for two centuries and gave the world the longest peace in history until the Pax Romana. About the middle of the Persian empire, Nehemiah, the last great political figure in the Old Testament, appeared. The Persian and the Roman empires were far more similar than formerly realized.

The Persian peace brought in one of the greatest periods of commercial expansion. They introduced an international language (Aramaic), rapid communications and good roads. They also put coinage on an international basis. In the sphere of politics Persia was the first world government to attempt to bring different races and nation-

The great audience hall of Darius and Xerxes at Persepolis.
Oriental Institute of the University of Chicago

alities under a central government which assured to all the *rights* and *privileges* of government as well as its burdens. They allowed the various subject races and existing civilizations to go on side by side with their own. They even permitted the Jews to coin their own money! Furthermore Persia interfered as little as possible in local government matters. Alexander himself found the Persian system of government so excellent that he took over almost bodily the Persian policy of world empire and simply grafted on to it his own Hellenistic policies.

The Persians' respect for truth and honor and their humane and chivalrous character was the secret of their nation's success. Their kings might lack these qualities, but the subject states of the empire seldom suffered seriously as most of the Persian subordinates were true to Persian ideals. The Persian's diplomatic and commercial language was Aramaic, not Persian! Thus Aramaic became one of the world's influential languages. Its inscriptions are found as far east as India. In Roman times the Levant had a renaissance of this language, which was then called Syriac, and it replaced Greek. The Persians were the founders of religious freedom on a world basis. Note that the Jews speak well only of the Persian empire. Rome returned to many of the Persian practices.

Many of the features of good government which these Persians introduced are those which we have often thought of as America's unique contribution to world history. We should be doing far more than we are in the light of over two thousand years of international history and especially in 1900 years of the teachings of Jesus Christ. The Persians deserve far more credit in world history than they have received. Unfortunately, too often the Greeks have

The ruins of Persepolis, a city established by Darius I and destroyed by Alexander the Great. *Oriental Institute of the University of Chicago*

been their historians, and your bitter enemy seldom speaks well of you.

Now let us return to the days of Cyrus. In antiquity the nations who were successful in war brought home to their capital city the chief idols of the conquered peoples as the major prize of victory. Thus mighty Babylon held the world's largest collection of gods in antiquity. When Cyrus conquered that empire he completely reversed this policy. He told all the conquered peoples to come to Babylon and take home their national gods. With Israel there was no idol, but the temple vessels taken away by Nebuchadnezzar were returned to Jerusalem in the care of Shesh-bazzar, fourth son of Jehoiachin. Under Darius, the Persian government even helped bear the expense of erecting Israel's new temple.

Cyrus brought Israel's seventy years of captivity to an end and permitted them to erect a new temple. All Jews who desired it could return to the promised land. The poor, however, were those chiefly interested in returning. Many other Israelite captives had entered business and made good. They financed the restoration of church and state but they stayed behind in the banking world of Babylonia. This is duplicated in the experience of modern Israel. It is financed by Jews, who prefer to remain in the country where they operate their business. The story of these first returnees under Cyrus was exactly the antithesis of Joshua's days. The history immediately following both the Exodus and the Exile was difficult but the Exodus was followed by the glory of the Conquest. The Exile, however, simply faded away.

The new temple was completed and dedicated in 515 B.C. A unique passover feast was observed in which the Exodus and the Exile were blended into a common me-

morial. The old-timers who had seen the glorious temple
of Solomon wept at the sight of this new commonplace
shrine. But it was the only one of Jerusalem's three temples that God did not destroy! How did it pass out of
the picture? Herod the Great decided to completely re-
make the city of Jerusalem exactly as we are doing with
our metropolitan areas. So he talked the temple clergy
into tearing down this antiquated little chapel and replacing it with a magnificent temple which would be one
of the wonders of the whole world.

Two outstanding figures dominate the picture of the
restoration. Nehemiah, cupbearer to Artaxerxes Longi-
manus, was the political figure. He was one who put
church above state. The Persian king gave him permission
to return to Jerusalem and administer the political situa-
tion there. He rebuilt the walls of Jerusalem approximately
150 years after Nebuchadnezzar had destroyed them. This
action, done with Persia's blessing, finally restored Israel to
its beloved capital — making Jerusalem again both a political and religious unit. The land that it actually controlled,
however, was a tiny principality not over twenty miles in
any direction. Later, maladministration in Jerusalem
brought Nehemiah back a second time as governor.

Ezra was the last religious genius in the Old Testament. Nehemiah 8:1-8 introduces us to his work and influence. He is called "the scribe" even though he was a
lineal descendant in the line of the high priest. The Bible
expert now became more important than the priestly tech-
nician at the altar. The introduction of the Bible school
teacher into the modern church program is a step forward
similar to that of the office of scribe of the restoration.
All Israel was gathered to Ezra and he read to them the
law of Moses and expounded it. This Bible must be at

the heart of the nation's life and Ezra saw to its exact enforcement. No Bible, no Israel! Ezra was also probably one of Israel's major historians for the books of Chronicles are most likely his composition. He probably did editorial work on other books but this can only be conjecture.

Also at this time the Samaritan schism was completed when Sanballat built a new temple on Mt. Gerizim for his son-in-law who was grandson of the Jewish high priest at Jerusalem. The Bible of these Samaritans consisted only of the Pentateuch. This period of the restoration is now being excavated by the archaeologists at Jerusalem, Mt. Gerizim and Shechem. After Ezra and Nehemiah Palestine disappears from history until the time of Alexander the Great.

It was the Exile which finally demonstrated to Israel that the Bible and the Sabbath were the two unique visible symbols of their faith. Since Jerusalem was the only place where the nation's temple could legitimately be located, the exiles were unable to carry on any sacrificial service in Babylon. That left them with only the Bible for worship; and in their loneliness and tragedy they drew this Bible to their hearts and appreciated it as never before in their history. The priests had originally performed two tasks, the sacrificial service and Bible teaching. Now they had only Bible teaching. This Book now meant so much to the common man that the priests and Levites had to move over and allow laymen of any tribe to teach the Bible. Thus the office of Scribe was created. Now any man could be a Bible scholar. Jesus Christ, the best scholar of them all, was from the tribe of Judah. Thus in the Exile the religious service was built around the Bible, and the synagogue service was created. So soul-satisfying was it that after the temple was rebuilt in Jerusalem the synagogue service continued to flourish even there. By the time of Jesus there were as many synagogues in Jerusalem as churches in a similar sized city today. Even today the Protestant Church patterns its worship service after that of the synagogue of the Exile.

Just as the Bible was uniquely appreciated in exilic and post-exilic days so was the Sabbath. It became so ingrained in Jewish life that the New Testament Church of Jerusalem, before that city's destruction in A.D. 70, seems to have kept both the Jewish and the Christian Sabbaths. One of today's greatest tragedies in church life is that intensive Bible study is now only a minor feature in many congregations. A second tragedy is that to many church members the morning of the Christian Sabbath is a *holy day*, but the remainder of that day is a *holiday!*

And yet never in history was there such a wealth of new information available for Bible study as now and never was the Sabbath more needed! Like the Jerusalem that crucified Christ we take our Bible and our Sabbath "seriously"; but also like Jerusalem we use them both just as *we please* and not as *God commands*.

Today many a denomination is over-emphasizing liturgy. A study of the book of Joel is a good antidote to this exaggeration. In Babylon some of the exiles thought that if they could get back to Jerusalem and rebuild the temple that then for them the millennium would be present. They did return, they did rebuild that temple; but then they had to learn that a temple is not enough. A great locust invasion swept over Palestine and everything green was eaten up even to the bark of the fig tree. Thus there was no food for the animals and they died.

Now there was a temple but there was nothing for sacrifice. They had to learn that there is something infinitely more important than the temple and the temple ritual. God revealed this to them in the promise of the Holy Spirit who is at the heart of worship. "And it shall come to pass afterward, that I will pour out my Spirit upon all flesh; and your sons and your daughters shall prophesy, your old men shall dream dreams, your young men shall see visions; and also upon the servants and upon the hand-maids in those days will I pour out my Spirit" (Joel 2:28-29). This is one of the rare promises in the Old Testament that deals with the third person of the Trinity. It was so prominent, however, that Peter instantly recalled it on the day of Pentecost.

The one venture in the United Nations where the most bitter enemies work hand in hand is in the world locust control. This ancient plague is also a modern one. In 125 B.C. a locust plague in the Roman colonies of North Africa brought death to over 800,000 persons. In sections of Africa today 75 to 100 per cent of crops are lost to locusts. The average yearly loss approaches $50,000,000. It is not uncommon to see swarms of locusts covering an area of 200 square miles. Such a unit would contain millions and millions of these insects. In flight they often shut out the sun. They make long flights and swarms have been seen over the Atlantic Ocean 1500 miles west of Africa. The 1930 locust invasion of the Sinai desert occupies a fascinating chapter in C. S. Jarvis, *Three Deserts.* Here are a few lines. "At this stage of the campaign we were dealing not only with the small black hopper locusts that had just hatched from the eggs, but also with fresh swarms that suddenly arrived from Arabia during the short breathing space that elapsed between the laying of the eggs and incubation. This meant that the whole of Sinai — an area as big as Scotland — was literally infested with the insects and the situation was complicated by the fact that they were in all stages. In one spot a gang of men would be employed digging and ploughing in an egg area; five miles away flame gunners would be engaged in burning out swarms of mature locusts; while close beside them would be a long line of workmen hastily digging a trench across the advance of a mass of five-day-old black hoppers."* When such a locust invasion was over in Joel's day, the temple would be practically useless for months for virtually no growing thing would be left for the services.

After the Exile Israel was done with idols of wood, stone and clay — things fashioned by the hand of man. But some 200 years later the Greeks would teach many of their descendants the greater idolatry of philosophy, the same kind of idolatry which many church people practice today either consciously or unconsciously. Another great lesson learned by the most saintly of the Jewish exiles in Babylonia was the necessity for foreign missions. This missionary effort, however, was at its best in Asia Minor and Paul profited from the work of the Jewish missionaries there. The final lesson that the Exile taught Israel was that the *nation* could never be the Messiah. He must be a person. And the noblest of their children longed for that experience which God granted unto Simeon when he took the Christ child in his arms and blessed God, saying, "Now lettest thou thy servant depart, Lord, According to thy word, in peace; For mine eyes have seen thy salvation, Which thou hast prepared before the face of all peoples; A light for revelation to the Gentiles, And the glory of thy people Israel" (Luke 2:29-32).

* * * *

*Quoted by permission from *Three Deserts* by C. S. Jarvis, published by John Murray, Ltd., London.

For detailed archaeological data, see W. F. Albright, *The Biblical Period from Abraham to Ezra*, Chapter X; and *From the Stone Age to Christianity*, Chapter VI. For locust material see, C. S. Jarvis, *Three Deserts*, Chapter XIV, "Annual Report of the Smithsonian Institute" 1944, pp. 331 ff. and *The National Geographic*, Dec. 1915, pp. 511-550.

The Spiritual Drought of
Intertestament Times and Today

The Spiritual Drought of Intertestament Times and Today

A limestone offering tray which stood before an Astarte idol.
Such worship was as empty as this tray.

The Old Testament is not the history of the Jews. It
is the *history of Revelation*. It is the story of God's self-
disclosure and His good purpose for man, whom He made
in His own likeness and for whose redemption He gave
His own Son. *God* is the *hero* of the Old Testament. Abraham, Moses, David, Isaiah, etc. are only *minor* figures in

the Old Testament. But these are men like ourselves and we are too often more interested in them than the God whom they worship. This volume has been a study of Old Testament saints and sinners — minor characters of the Bible. A companion volume is now being written that will concentrate on the *God of the Old Testament*, whom we all underestimate and whom we all too seldom try to understand and appreciate. Although He is also the God of the New Testament we take Him much more seriously there.

Since the Old Testament is a history of Revelation we find that it deals only with those periods when God is revealing some new truth or re-emphasizing former truth. Thus there is approximately a four-century blank between Genesis and Exodus and about the same between the Old Testament and the New Testament. Although some scholars have theorized that considerable Old Testament material is located in that four-century period before the birth of Christ, the literature from Qumran and other archaeological data have eliminated most of this debatable material. Only a minor amount comes from these centuries.

In terms of secular history the intertestament period witnessed the death of the Persian empire at the hands of Alexander the Great. His empire collapsed with his death and Ptolemaic Egypt took over Palestine. Approximately 200 B.C. it passed into the hands of the Seleucids at Antioch. Then one of those rulers, Antiochus Epiphanes, tried to exterminate Judaism. Palestine revolted and secured its religious freedom in 165 B.C., and shortly after it was granted political independence. The Maccabaean rulers, however, followed the tragic Greek pattern of government and in 63 B.C. Rome took over Palestine and subleased it to Herod the Great. This happened early in those military power struggles which ended in the creation of the Roman empire with Augustus Caesar as the first ruler. These wars were in those days the same horrors that World Wars I and II were to us. That Mediterranean world so longed for peace that when Augustus brought this into actuality it was said of him that his deeds outdid the prayers and expectations of all humanity! But it is not so much the secular history of the intertestament period that we are interested in as it is the religious and philosophical story of that time.

Although there was little new revelation after 400 B.C. there was a rash of new *heresies* springing up everywhere! In Palestine this was a secularizing period quite similar to our own age. Greek culture had burst like a pent-up flood in Palestine after Alexander the Great, although it had long been a minor influence there. Many of the Israelite priesthood fell for this pagan culture and grafted it into their Old Testament creed, making an impossible hybrid creed which Christ had to destroy. The Maccabees usurped the high priestly office although they were good enough to promise that they would abdicate when the Messiah came. Alexander Jannaeus was a typical Greek king and even worse. He could decorate his palace garden with 800 crosses upon which some of his own Jewish supporters were crucified. Meanwhile, their wives and children were killed as they looked on. The Jewish authorities who crucified Christ were only normal intertestament politicians. Not even Christ Himself could persuade these people into the kingdom. They clamored not only for His death but also for their own and by A.D. 70 Israel was gone and the Church had replaced her as God's evangelistic agent. These centuries also marked the composition of the Apocrypha,

Top: Arabic fortress erected over a section of the palace of
Herod the Great in Jerusalem. *Kelso*
Bottom: The tall, mended jars hold the scrolls found in Cave 1.
The cooking pot on the shelf above is also from Qumran and
dates to about the time of Christ. *Kelso*

those books rejected by Jews and Protestants but which form an integral part of the Catholic Bible.

God had chosen Israel to evangelize the world. Abraham received that assignment somewhere about 1900 B.C. Israel failed completely, even after a second chance in the Babylonian exile. She became simply another pagan nation like Sodom and Gomorrah and as such she had to go. As Lot and family were spared so were some true believers, but Israel's days as God's evangelists were over. The horror of today is that the Christian Church is seeing the close of the 1900 years since Christ ordered *her* to *evangelize the world*; and the modern Church is emphasizing everything under heaven except what is the only purpose of her existence, i.e. foreign missions.

There were a few spiritual Jews, however, who did not bow the knee to the new pagan Greek Baal philosophy. These were those who were true to Christ in the gospel narratives. The really influential Jewish element, however, that carried the Old Testament in their heart were the missionary Jews. They were key businessmen in Asia Minor, but their primary concern was to evangelize their pagan customers and neighbors. So successful was their work that in many of the places where Paul visited congregations of evangelistic Jews were already there and Paul had only to demonstrate to them that Jesus was the Messiah for whom they were looking, and they became Christians.

This intertestament period produced the Essenes whom we now know at first hand from the wealth of manuscripts and artifacts coming from the excavations at Qumran. They represented the old priesthood who considered the Maccabees such blasphemers that they must abandon the holy temple in Jerusalem, go down to the

Dead Sea valley, and wait for God to work a miracle similar to that in Sinai. To the Essenes Jerusalem was as wicked as the Egypt of Moses. They concentrated on Bible study and this was carried on twenty-four hours a day. But in it all they missed the Messiah and they refused to accept Jesus Christ when He came. They had even used exactly the same text (Isaiah 40:3 ff.) to justify their move to Qumran that John the Baptist used to introduce men to Christ. Alas those Bible students, like many today, missed their Christ, which is to miss their God as He was revealed in the flesh. The Essenes built their monastery on the shores of the same Dead Sea that now covers Sodom and Gomorrah. Sex and scholarship can use the same road to destruction though they have no dealings with one another as they walk the common road of rationalism.

I was one of the first archaeologists to visit Cave I at Qumran, and I have continued to follow all work there with interest. The following represent some of the unique finds at Qumran. This site is actually the forerunner of the Christian monastery although there is no chronological relationship. Although the rulers lived in the monastery complex, the community members lived in tents and caves scattered over an area about two miles north and south of the chapter house. Here at Qumran we also have an ideal opportunity to watch an ancient denomination grow, for we have the manuscripts they wrote through the years and these show the changes they made in their creed and their law codes.

Most helpful, of course, for Bible study is their wealth of Old Testament manuscripts. These are by far the oldest ever found, although in many cases some of the pages are in almost as good condition as when they were written. I never cease to thrill at the sight of some of these pages

Left: Nabataean tombs at Petra. *Kelso*

Below: The El-Khazneh Temple is carved in the rock cliff at the right in the rose-red canyons of Petra. © *Matson Photo Service*

which look as if the ink were hardly dry on the manuscript, although the last of their manuscripts was written approximately 1900 years ago. The problem of the Old Testament canon is also illuminated by these manuscripts. Every book of the Old Testament except Esther is illustrated by a complete book or a fragment of a book. If Esther were then written on a scroll along with other small books, as was the case with later manuscripts, then we cannot be certain that even it is missing since the other books are all present. To judge from the number of manuscripts preserved, their favorite books were Deuteronomy, Psalms and Isaiah. Daniel also presents a fair number of manuscripts as this book was highly influential in their doctrinal thinking. Some of these manuscripts at times represent slightly different texts and as a result of these variations Bible scholars for the first time in history can see how the textual variations crept in between the early Hebrew and Greek manuscripts.

The doctrinal works of the Essenes which deal in detail with their own beliefs light up many passages in the New Testament. We can now see better the details of the problems refuted by John's gospel and we now know that John's gospel must be dated very early, whereas most scholars have been dating it late. The Essenes also throw light on church government in the pastoral epistles, and their Pauline authorship is now easy to understand. In short, so much new light has come into the New Testament world that there is no need to date the authorship of any New Testament book after the destruction of Jerusalem in A.D. 70, or at the latest a few years after that.

Nowhere, however, does the work of the Essenes improve on the Old Testament. And since they rejected Christ as their Messiah they can contribute nothing to the

New Testament. To both Testaments they form a brilliant contrasting background which brings out the true uniqueness of Scripture. The significance of these new finds is demonstrated by the fact that there is already a large technical journal devoted exclusively to the publication of articles on all phases of the Dead Sea scrolls.

The Sadducees also came out of this intertestament period. Like the Essenes they were a small group but they did not seek seclusion. Instead they sought both political and religious power and they got both, even to crucifying their own Messiah. The Sadducees were a good blend of the modern liberal ecclesiastical politician and the big businessman. They also had their Ph.D.'s. They were such good logicians that they could at times hold a better doctrine of Scripture than the Pharisees and yet at the same time deny the doctrine of the resurrection in the Old Testament by the use of that same Scripture. Unfortunately, they were the losers in the Judaism that succeeded the destruction of the temple and thus the fine details of their theology have not been preserved.

The Pharisee is the man for you to watch when you read the New Testament for the modern Jew is in most instances his lineal descendant. And 1900 years have made little difference in the hard core of his philosophy. Christ has exactly the same problem today in winning the Jew that He had in winning the Pharisee and for the same reason. The Pharisee was omniscient. As a super rationalist he could theorize for you a Scripture answer for every minute problem of human existence. To appreciate a new and more accurate view of the gospels one should read them alongside of the Mishna. When the Jews rejected Jesus this is the book they produced as an antidote to the New Testament. Only when these two books are read side by side, then and only then will you see the vast difference between the Pharisee and Jesus.

From Adam and Eve up to the Sadducees and the Pharisees, too many people in every generation thought God's wisdom was only second to their own. And our generation likewise seems to consider itself a genius at remodeling God. But in every age as soon as men have tampered with Scripture they have already tampered with their own souls. That was the problem of so much of the Jewish world into which Christ came; and such a world saw no sin in crucifying its Messiah! Today, how many of us Christians show Christ the obedience He deserves? He is our *Saviour* but we refuse to crown Him *King*.

Epilogue

This book has been emphasizing that the big men of modern history are no greater and no better than the big men of the Old Testament. Also the general patterns in the histories of modern nations are quite similar to, though not identical with, those of Old Testament times. If space had permitted, it could have been shown that at heart every strata of society then and now is likewise fairly similar, although in externalities they be as far apart as east and west.

In my many travels in Europe, the Near East and America I have seen the same awful poverty that we read of in Scripture and which we dig up as archaeologists. I have also seen similar parallel levels from every other strata of society then and now. Archaeology and history have demonstrated that people are pretty much the same in all generations. The one and only overwhelming difference in all the world is that between those who worship the God of the Bible and those who reject Him; and time plays absolutely no essential part in that choice. The men of the Old Testament are our contemporaries. We should also be the contemporaries of Christ!

* * * *

For detailed archaeological data, see W. F. Albright, *From the Stone Age to Christianity,* Chapter VI.

Index